W9-AMQ-459

Happiness

on 7 Dollars a Week

A Formula for Living

Happiness

on 7 Dollars a Week

A Formula for Living

Harley B. Bernstein

Copyright © 2003 Harley B. Bernstein

All rights reserved. No part of this publication
may be reproduced or transmitted in any form or
by any means, electronic or mechanical, including
photocopy, digital imaging, recording, or any
information storage and retrieval system, without
permission in writing from the publisher, except
in the case of brief quotations embodied in
critical articles and reviews.

Published by Barstin Books
P.O. Box 407
Vienna, VA 22183

Library of Congress Cataloging-in-Publication Data

Bernstein, Harley B.,
Happiness on 7 Dollars a Week: A Formula for Living /
Harley B. Bernstein. — IST ed.

1. Self-Help - Death, Grief, Bereavement.   2. Happiness.
3. Motivational.   4. Self-Actualization (Psychology)
5. Spirituality (Religion)   I. Title.

ISBN: 0-9740264-0-9
Printed in the United States of America
October 2003

4 H 8 B 8 B

For More Information About
Happiness on 7 Dollars a Week
www.happyonseven.com

This book is dedicated to my mother, Rhoda,
to serve as a monument to her strength
and the love she had for her family.

Contents

Acknowledgements

It is with the utmost respect and deepest appreciation to acknowledge my father Al Bernstein for his lifetime commitment to helping others and his sincere efforts to communicate his ideals.

I also want to thank my wife Kari and daughter Marisa for their enthusiastic support during this long journey. I am most grateful to Laurie Szpot who believed in me and provided the heavy lifting of two full edits that shaped this book. A special thanks to my brothers: Bud Bernstein who offered artistic guidance to this novice writer and helped polish the final words presented; and Rick Bernstein who challenged me to not only capture Dad's character, but also our relationship. I thank Cathleen Griffin and Lucy Lapidus for their attention to detail in proofing this work. And, thank you to Miriam Bass for all her professional guidance.

For their patience in reading and critiquing several drafts of this book, I thank Heather Hallsey-Bernstein, Rich and Norma Behnke, Mark and Sue McCallister, and Jonathon Perrelli.

I would like to thank people who have touched my life and helped me to reach this day: (in order of appearance)

My teachers: Henry Isaacs, Regina Ruhlin, Phil Emery, Art Monk, Paul Murphy, Kim Novak, Dorothy Pratt, Bob Jones, Kenneth Schwartz and David Kalender. Thank you for raising the bar.

My lifetime friends: Scott Glass, Rob DeBurro, Steve Marcus, Steve McCool, Grant Lineberry, Gus and Debbie Amann, Gary and Nancy Beskow, Chris and Stacey Marchetti, Jeff and Pam

Marchetti, Jeff and Sandra Frederick, Ellen Slaughter, Denwood Bowling, Chuck and Loretta Kayser, Deedy Eisenson, Evie Stein, Fabian and Beth Rivelis, Danny and Jill Mayer, Tom and Debbie Berkley, Rich and Elana Plotnick, Gary and Lisa Shankman, Andy and Eileen Dudenhoeffer, Barry and Melissa Franks, and Stacy and Susanne Oshry. Thank you for being role models and sharing your lives with my family.

I am especially grateful to Warren and Myrna Sondon, Jodi Sondon-Anthony, and Wendy and Judah Katz for their love and assistance over the years; and the Striar family and the Striar Foundation of Bangor, Maine for supporting the first seven years of my education.

Note from the Author

The concepts presented in this book are based on insights acquired during countless discussions and hundreds of walks with my dad and from the volumes of his writing. I have tried to capture the example he sets and to present his philosophy in a simple manner from the perspective of a father's advice to his son. If this book presents my dad as anything other than the gentle and humble man he is, please remember that this is my impression of his beliefs and how he lives his life.

Happiness

on 7 Dollars a Week

A Formula for Living

Harley B. Bernstein

Like Father, Like Son

As a kid I loved walks with Dad. I still do. Dad has always taken walks with his three sons, generally one on one. It's his way of keeping up with what's going on in our lives. It's one of his passions.

Dad is also passionate about writing—more like obsessed. I remember many mornings, waking up early and going downstairs to the basement of our house on Lancaster Avenue in Bangor, Maine. I would find Dad writing in the furnace room. He would be seated at a simple folding table, under a single bulb with a pull string. A small, bright window near the ceiling at his back made him appear in silhouette. He would be writing, thinking, or sometimes even reading his own work in a whisper. He was working on a book entitled, *The Art of Living*. I wondered, *what secrets can be found in those pages?*

Dad's writing affected our family's routine. He wrote every morning, except Saturdays. This was the one day each week when he consciously took a break. Sundays were the toughest for us kids. We were asked to keep quiet until 10 a.m.—quite a feat. This allowed Dad to complete his session likely to have begun at 5 a.m. Then we would have breakfast with him and watch *Tom and Jerry*, followed by *The Three Stooges*.

Dad didn't like interruption unless, of course, we needed help with a problem. Then he would drop everything to talk with us. Generally, my oldest brother, Bud, reserved time during Dad's morning shave, mostly to discuss history or politics. During adolescence, Rick, the middle brother, spent a lot of time with him in the evenings. As for me, I liked to take early morning walks with Dad discussing anything and everything.

Almost everyone who comes in contact with Dad finds him to be a very patient listener and confidante. He always seems to have the right answer, as if he had already spent years pondering a specific problem or situation. It's likely he had.

There were many target dates over the years for the completion of Dad's written masterpiece—birthdays, anniversaries, you name it. They all came and went. He did manage to finish a couple of other books on the subjects of politics and philosophy. Still, I wondered if Dad would ever complete this project. But even as a kid, I knew one thing: If he didn't, I'd grow up someday and finish that book.

The opportunity arrived in the fall of 1997 when I learned in a phone call with Dad that he was about to throw away nearly fifty years of his work. He felt it had become too cumbersome, and he had decided to work on another book.

To me, this was unthinkable.

Had he lost his mind? I wondered. *Maybe.*

I had him ship it to me.

Within a week, over four thousand handwritten pages, boxed for destruction, arrived at my door. *The Art of Living*, Dad's unfinished manuscript, was now available. I stuffed it in my closet for safekeeping. The sheer volume was overwhelming and I wasn't sure when I'd even read it.

From time to time, when we were together on walks, I would remind Dad of my intentions. He always seemed amused with the idea and humored me in my belief, not really wanting to burden me with the editing effort required. I cherished walks with Dad. It was the conversation and the interaction that I enjoyed. To this day, I still find that walks with Dad are great opportunities to revisit my childhood, where any subject can be discussed and most problems solved. Dad is my conscience, my spiritual advisor, and my best friend.

Dad's obsession with writing continued over the next few years; it ended abruptly in July of 2000. One week before the occasion of my parents' 50th wedding anniversary, Mom's cancer was back. There had never been any guarantee that breast cancer, in remission for two years, would not return. It did. This time as a brain tumor. The anniversary party was on hold. There would be no celebration. Dad's writing stopped. What terrible timing. As if cancer could ever be convenient.

Mom had suspicions the cancer had returned. Yet she thought she could manage it, like everything else. She would fight. Her concern grew until one day she was forced to check it out.

Mom drove herself to her doctor's appointment. She received the news alone. When she was late getting home, Dad had my brother Rick drive him to Mom's doctor. They found her talking with him. Dad could tell something was wrong. She was standing with a balled-up tissue in her hands. Her eyes were red and welled with tears, yet Mom remained composed.

My telephone rang that July day around noon. It was Dad, all choked up, calling to explain that the news he had wasn't good. A minute later, Mom was on the line assuring me she was okay. Shocked and afraid, I followed her lead refusing to communicate fear. She wasn't panicked. I wouldn't panic either. I played the role so well that I couldn't even manage to say *I love you* before we said goodbye.

Mom was a rock. She never complained. To me, she'd always been indestructible.

At 3:00 a.m. she might be calling United Airlines, booking flights for a family reunion, or, to our delight, baking the best brownies in the world, even though we knew they came from a Duncan Hines box. Always doting on her grandchildren, she'd play games with them for hours. She would never die, or so I believed.

Dad, always the optimist, stood by to comfort her. Later, I learned he'd been quietly prepared for the worst. Their strength was comforting, but I should have been comforting them. What could I do?

That night I sat alone in my study. I pulled a photo album off the shelf. Looking at pictures from an earlier day, Mom was so vibrant. All I could do was shake my head. And then it hit me. Perhaps I could find the answers in Dad's book. There it was, sitting on the closet floor, right in front of me.

Mom's illness and rapid decline served as the ultimate test for Dad's beliefs, as well as a catalyst for me. It allowed me to imagine a world without them. I imagined reading Dad's book after he was gone; it was not comforting at all, not the least bit nostalgic. *What if I had questions?* Missing this chance was a sin. *What was I thinking?*

I now had a new course. I immediately began reading Dad's manuscript and considered the process of completing his work.

Meanwhile, Dad would need a lot of time to repair his broken heart. He only slowly discovered that fifty years of marriage couldn't be conveniently placed on a shelf for safekeeping, like the pages of a book. No. He would need to confront a lifetime of shared memories, love and pain, including the final chapter.

I would need to complete Dad's work, but in my own way. Like father, like son, I had found a new obsession. I would write a story that would complement the hundreds of walks and thousands of conversations we've had over the years. I would capture the words of his heart and the wisdom gained from his experience.

Join us in this series of walks, father with son. I'm mostly reporting his story, covering subjects such as fear, appreciation, acceptance, and adjustment each through the prism of one conversation and one walk. These conversations become the building blocks—with Dad's spirituality the glue—that demonstrate a remarkable life-long secret to happiness.

Most of our walks take place on familiar grounds in Maine, surroundings that comforted us while we tried to comfort Mom. Our deepest prayers could not restore Mom's health. Nor could they support the foundation of Dad's happiness. I would discover that, in time, Dad's formula would work for him again. Even under these circumstances, he would find purpose to his life and regain the peace of mind and happiness that were being lost to despair.

Walk 1 – Can Anybody Really Change?

I looked at Dad slumped peacefully in a chair as we sat just outside Mom's hospital room. His hands were folded across his chest with his fingers interlocked. This was Dad, so calm, adrift in his private thoughts, always the picture of peace. I sat on his left. Even with his hearing aids, it was still his better side.

Dad, I said, breaking the silence. I'm reading your book.

He sat up. His eyes opened wide. "You don't say. What do you think?"

I think we've got a lot of work ahead of us.

His natural grin became a laugh. Then he got up and went to check on Mom. I remained in the lounge, which was simply furnished with four chairs and a coffee table covered with dated magazines. Like her room, it seemed empty and cold.

Mom's tumor had been removed a couple of weeks earlier, but the prognosis wasn't good, perhaps six months. A regimen of radiation treatments had begun. The side effects were headaches caused by a buildup of fluid. As a result, a shunt had to be placed in her brain to relieve the pressure. Mom was generally conscious and alert, but speaking was very difficult for her.

Dad spent most of his time at the hospital, assisted by my brothers, Rick and Bud. I shuttled between Virginia and Maine every two weeks. Dad and I spent hours sitting beside Mom's bed or in the lounge across from her room. We had plenty of time to talk about Mom and the concepts of his book. I knew that working on his book was a project we both needed, and it seemed to help pass the time.

While visiting, I stayed with Dad at their apartment. The house they had owned, the one with Dad's little basement writing studio, had been sold the year after I'd left for college. The apartment was small yet organized. Mom ran a tight ship. Her favorite room was the kitchen. It was a little cramped, but that didn't seem to bother her. Whether it was having tea with Dad, cooking until two in the morning for one of our many family gatherings, or scouring the newspaper for coupons, this is where she spent most of her time. She even had a small TV on the counter so she wouldn't miss a minute of the Boston Red Sox. On Sundays Dad watched *Sixty Minutes*, and Mom waited patiently at the kitchen table for their weekly game of Scrabble.

I was reading *The Bangor Daily News*, while Dad prepared a snack: a glass of pineapple juice and rye toast with olive oil. I happened to glance at the refrigerator and noticed a card attached with a magnet. It was a birthday card for Mom from over a month ago.

Dear Rhoda,

To the most ecstatically beautiful, exciting and inspiring lady in the world:

HAPPY BIRTHDAY!

I love you with all my heart, with all my soul, with all my strength, with all my might, and with all my mind.

Love and devotion,

Your true love,

Al

I could remember this same message on every card Dad gave her, no matter what the occasion. It was part of his tradition that included a box of fancy cashews and Fannie Farmer truffles. I think the truffles were actually *his* favorite.

Dad saw me reading the card.

"That's right," he offered, reading my mind. "I still write the same old corny stuff.

"I did this since the early days of our marriage. The funny thing was that after a while, Rhoda would write cards that were similar to mine," Dad continued.

"She'd say, *I can write this now, but when you lose your hair, you're out of here.*

"Even later on, when I had to get bifocals, trifocals and hearing aids, I'd ask her, *Am I still acceptable?*

"Oh yeah but when you lose your hair...

"Hah, hah, hah," he laughed in an exaggerated manner.

"She'd always respond in kind, right down to all my heart, soul, strength, might and mind, but she'd always leave one out. And I'd say, Hey, you missed one.

"Come on, she'd say, *it's a whole package. It still counts.*"

Then he paused to think about it for a minute. He looked down at his hands and collected himself.

"The package deal wouldn't have covered me, though, if I lost my hair. Then all bets were off," he said, lightening things up again.

Would the deal really have been over, I pried, or was it open to negotiation?

"Nope. No negotiation. That would have been it. Period.

"You see, my father and my uncles were all bald at an early age. The comical part was that Rhoda should have been more worried for herself. Except for her mother, most of the women in her family had hair challenges of their own."

I looked at him and thought, *what will he do without her? Who will care for him? Who will cook for him? Buy his clothes? Keep him company?*

Dad continued with the evening routine of preparing his morning breakfast. He carefully measured out a half-cup of bran and a half-cup of oats and soaked them in water overnight to remove the acid. Once that had been tended to, we headed for the living room. Dad kicked back in the La-Z-Boy.

Completely relaxed, he folded his arms across his chest and closed his eyes. It would be only a matter of seconds before Dad would be asleep; I quickly confirmed a 6:30 a.m. appointment with him for our customary morning walk to talk about his book.

I woke up the next morning in the small den that doubled as a guest bedroom. While getting dressed, I noticed a letter lying on the desk. It was a draft of the speech Mom had planned to read at the anniversary party.

I read the part where she thanked everyone for coming, people from as far away as California, Florida, Toronto, Montreal and Boston. She made particular reference to Warren, her brother, who meant the world to her, and to Andoretta, her best friend since playing together in their old neighborhood in Montreal when they were seven years old.

Then she wrote:

> *I feel very lucky and blessed to have had the companionship and love of my dear husband Al for the past fifty years. I am also very fortunate to have shared so closely in the lives of my wonderful children, Bud, Rick and Heather, and Harley and Kari. And, I am most thankful for the precious gift of my grand-children, Josh, Adam, and Marisa. You have all made my life and this day very special. We love you all.*

I guess Dad left it there for her to read at a future celebration.

I set the letter down. I was ready for a walk. Then I heard Dad poking around. I peeked out and saw him standing in front of the mirror in the living room in a white crewneck T-shirt. He adjusted his gold-rimmed glasses.

Seeing me in the reflection he said, "I'm almost ready to go."

At age seventy-three, he still looked remarkably young. His light brown hair had thinned some on the top and grayed a bit on the sides. His eyebrows were bushy and inquisitive. He styled his wet hair by combing back the strands over his head as he continued to prepare himself. Then he put on a plaid short-sleeved dress shirt and buttoned it up. It would only be another minute or so.

Let's go, I said, with my usual impatience and headed for the door.

Dad tapped the front pockets of his pants with his hands to check for his keys and wallet. Then he tapped his back pocket to make sure he had a pen and his *little black book,* as he calls it.

Dad always carries a pen and a small black notebook with him. It's about the size of a stack of index cards. He likes the ones with three rings so pages can be added or removed easily. He took it out for a minute and glanced at a couple of pages.

What do you use that for? I asked.

"Self-improvement," he answered. "I'm not perfect. Nobody is. My little black book helps keep me conscious of the changes I'm trying to make in my life. I like to track my progress so I can understand what went wrong and work on a corrective strategy. I probably take three to four pages of notes each week for the specific issues I'm working on. I also use it to write down thoughts that come up during the day or to note things I want to cover at a later time. It's so easy to forget these days."

How long have you been carrying one around with you?

"It all started when I was in the Service. My memory was so good in those days that if I had a thought or idea, and I didn't have time at the moment to explore it I could just put it in my mind and pick it up the next day. Well, one time when I was in Germany, I had a fascinating thought. Later, it just disappeared and I never found it again. To this day, I still don't know what it was. Who knows, it may have been the answer to world peace! And let me tell you, this really bothered me. That's when I began carrying loose sheets of paper with me in my pockets.

"When I returned to the United States, my first books were notepads. But I couldn't easily pull pages out or replace them. Now I've got a system.

"Look at this," he exclaimed, as he pulled it out, demonstrating how the rings opened and closed.

"Rhoda used to kid me about my notebook. It was always there, and I never hid it from her. I think she looked at it a couple of times and found it a complete waste of time."

Pretty dull, huh? I said.

"Yeah, that's right, pretty dull," he repeated goodnaturedly. "You know an amazing thing? There were times when I wrote about Rhoda and my dealings with her. It's a lucky thing she never discovered this, or my strategy with her could have been blown."

I think you carry your little black book as a security blanket, I jabbed.

"You're right. In fact, I remember one time when I worked at Viner Music Company and left it there overnight. I found it Monday, but being without it wrecked my whole weekend."

Then Dad put his hand to his ear to test the batteries in his hearing aids. There was a little buzz. At last, he was ready.

It was still early, about a quarter to seven, and there was very little traffic on Husson Avenue. We walked up the block to Broadway and waited for the light. This stretch of Broadway isn't one of Bangor's most attractive. It mostly houses fast food restaurants, gas stations, a car dealership and a shopping center. We headed out Broadway, away from the "Miracle Mile," towards the high school.

Then Dad asked in his Downeast twang, "Well, Young Fella, what's on your mind today?"

Your book, I readily responded.

He pulled out his little black book, flipped through some pages and found the points he wanted to cover.

"So, you're reading my book," he said, smiling.

That's right.

I was curious about the research he'd done. So I asked him several questions.

Where did you get all this material? Are they all your ideas? Did you read a lot?

"I do not consider myself to be a scholar," Dad said quietly, "Some people do no end of reading with no end of books. I found I enjoyed reading so much that it slowed me down. I couldn't just read a book start to finish. I'd read something interesting and I couldn't help but thinking about it exhaustively. I could barely finish a book. Nowadays, I don't have time for both reading and thinking. So I've chosen thinking: contemplation, meditation and theosophy. In my early days, I would jot down as many as thirty to forty pages of notes at a time."

I wasn't exactly sure what Dad meant by theosophy, but he later told me that it was spiritual meditation for seeking universal truth. He claimed to have spent a minimum of two hours a day for over twenty years searching for such truths.

"In the book, I've offered a formula for success, happiness and peace of mind." He paused and gathered his thoughts. "The real answer is found not just by reading the words, but by following its path and living life."

I knew Dad walked this path. Was it possible for me to capture and document his method for others?

"Still, there are a few things you'll need to know: You've got to read the material with an open mind, to be open to all constructive possibilities and truths. You've got to consider ideas, methods, lifestyles and beliefs that may be different from your own. You've got to be open to the risk.

"Are you willing to do this?" he asked.

Before I could answer, we reached the corner of Essex Street and Lancaster Avenue. I looked down the street beyond the row of cedars hiding our old driveway. There it was: my childhood home. I loved that place.

It wasn't fancy. It was a small Cape Cod with white siding and black shutters. A silver maple tree branched out in all directions in the front yard, its leaves generally green, until the wind exposed their shinier underbellies. It had grown, like the rest of the trees, but everything else was much the same as we had left it, everything except the lamppost on the front walk, which had fallen over. The back yard was shaded by a towering sugar maple, likely over a hundred years old. As kids, my brothers and I enjoyed climbing it. In the fall its color was a brilliant cascade of orange, yellow and red. And when the leaves fell we'd rake piles and build forts, taller than ourselves.

Dad and I stopped directly in front of the house. I envisioned the small bedroom upstairs, under the eaves, which I had shared with Rick. I gazed at the big picture window with white curtains. Mom had that window added so that she could look out into the world. I now struggled to see in from the street.

I pictured Dad, writing in the basement. I could hear the dueling sounds of Rick banging out *Maple Leaf Rag* on the upright piano in the living room and Bud upstairs in his bedroom playing Sly and the Family Stone on his stereo. And I could almost smell one of Mom's homemade pies, baked with the fresh blueberries we had picked from the field behind the house. I imagined her smiling face, looking out the back window over the kitchen sink, watching me play.

I also noticed the little "B" centered on the wrought iron grill of the front storm door. Mom's favorite rhododendron still grew in the flowerbed and an overgrown lilac bush flourished on the side. In the spring it would bloom lavender with the sweetest smell I had ever known.

My parents sold this house almost twenty years ago, but I still considered the people who'd bought it the *new* owners. They'd added a garage, which blocked the view of the field behind the house. Except for the broken lamp along the front walk, the house appeared to be in good condition.

We continued down the street, passing Mrs. Bridges' old white farmhouse with the attached red barn. Mrs. Bridges died a few years ago at the age of ninety-eight.

I only knew Mrs. Bridges as the little old lady that lived alone until one day when our paths crossed while she was getting her mail at the side of the road. She described the days when there weren't any roads out here, only trails for horses and carriages. She told me that she'd had relatives twenty-five miles away in Newport, Maine, and that she and her family had routinely visited them in the summer, on foot. They'd start walking just before sunrise and arrive before dark.

Now that was a walk. She may have been small and walked with a cane, but after that conversation, I never again thought of her as a little old lady.

The land adjoining Mrs. Bridges' house had been sold and developed. Two new houses had been recently built, completely foreign to my memory. It seemed an invasion, and I shook my head.

They couldn't have done that, I thought. *Didn't they realize that this was where Rick and I played baseball in the summer? Didn't they know that in the winter, melting snow pooled in between the snow banks and refroze, making a skating rink the size of a park?*

Then I realized, for everything that had remained the same, something else had changed.

"I have some questions for you," Dad said, breaking the silence.

He raised his eyebrows, prompting a response.

Questions?

"Yes, questions. Questions such as: Can you objectively assess a new idea? Are you able to recognize your own biases and motives? Can you understand other perspectives and be reflective, yet not be poisoned by gossip or unproven state-ments?"

That's quite a task, I countered. You're talking about changing a person's thoughts and habits. Is that even possible? Can anybody really change?

"I asked myself that very question when I first started writing," Dad said.

And what was the answer?

"At the time, I was very much influenced by Professor Adriance, one of my sociology teachers. He claimed:

> *Man is one hundred percent the result of our heritage, our genes and chromosomes, the books we read, the people we meet, what we're taught, and the influence of our parents and friends. We're like puppets on a string. The little bit of so-called free will we do have to change is negligible."*

Do you still believe this?

"No," Dad answered, without hesitation. "I came to realize—in fact, it was Rabbi Gordon who told me:

> *If you really believe that people have no free will, then there's no real possibility for creativity. If you're creative it's because your culture made you that way. If you're destructive—say a criminal—you can blame it on society. You can justify anything without conscience or responsibility. With this view you lose all sense of purpose and meaning in life,* he said, convincingly.

"So I came to believe that even though it may not be easy, people do have the free will to change. Without this fundamental belief, nothing else matters."

If it's so difficult for people to change, then why did you even bother writing this book? I challenged.

"Look," Dad answered humbly, "I've already accepted the fact that the only benefit that I might get from writing this book is self-expression. I'm satisfied knowing that even if the only person this book helps is me, or you for that matter, it will have all been worthwhile," he said with a smile of contentment.

Then why should anybody bother reading it? I cross-examined.

"As I said, I don't expect people to make major changes. What I hope to accomplish is modification. Even the slightest modification can make all the difference."

That's it? I asked skeptically. Modification?

"What's wrong with modification?" Dad asked. "Not everyone has the discipline of a Mahatma Gandhi, nor should that be expected. I haven't changed that much in my lifetime, yet I've witnessed the difference between having peace of mind and not having peace of mind, just from some very subtle modifications. *The Art of Living* is modification. That's the recipe. Use whatever part you need. The choice is yours."

Our walk had almost brought us back to our starting point. We had just reached the last stop on my old paper route, *Momma Baldacci's*. The restaurant is a Bangor landmark, attracting visiting movie stars, well-known athletes, the Kennedys, and regular folks like us. But the real beauty of the place is the family itself. Grandparents, parents and children all worked side by side over the years. This is a genuine American success story of an immigrant family. One of their kids, John, is now Maine's Governor.

As we passed the restaurant, I asked Dad about the ability to change others.

"I learned a long time ago that it's nearly impossible to get other people to change," Dad said. "It's hard enough to change myself. What makes me think I can change anyone else? Rather, I believe that people change when they want to change. So I limit the demands I place on others. When I do seek change in others, the best I hope for is to influence or modify them."

And that's where we stopped. Today's lecture was over. If prompted, Dad would have been happy to continue, but I was content with our progress for the day.

"You know," Dad said, "since Rhoda's illness I've been pressed into managing the household finances and I've made a slight modification."

Really? What's that?

"Well, with the added responsibility, I've decided to give myself a raise." He paused for effect and grinned like a child who'd snuck an extra cookie. "That's right. I've raised my allowance from seven dollars a week to ten."

*I couldn't believe it. For all those years, **the happiest man I knew had an allowance of seven dollars a week!***

Walk 2 – Digging Your Way Out

⟝⟝⟝ Dad was twelve years old when his father, Charlie, disappeared.

A lender by trade, Charlie traveled the East Coast with a novel pitch: borrow money to buy cars. On a gray December day in 1939, Charlie boarded a steamship in Boston bound for New York. The boat arrived as scheduled, but Charlie didn't. They found his suitcase in his cabin. His bed hadn't been slept in. It was not known whether he'd committed suicide, was a victim of foul play, or had deserted his family. Within a year of his disappearance, a court of law concluded—without discovering a body—that Charles Bernstein had died. This equitable solution allowed a widow with six children, four still living at home, including a newborn, to collect on several small life insurance policies.

A few days before Charlie's disappearance, Dad thought he had seen his father in a daze. The night before Charlie left for his trip, Dad remembers his father entering his bedroom, a room Dad shared with his twin brother Bob and their older brother Seldon. He'd come to take his suitcase out of their closet before the brothers went to sleep to avoid disturbing them later. Early the next morning, Charlie came to their room again.

"I thought, *maybe he'd forgotten something,*" Dad said. "But I didn't open my eyes. I think he came in for one last look."

Dad vividly remembers his mother gathering the kids and reporting the news.

"When she told us he was gone, she asked us never to discuss it. There was no visible mourning in our house. I never saw my mother cry. No tears were shed by me or any of my three brothers."

How was this possible?

"I don't think it was denial," Dad answered, with very little emotion. "I just felt that even though I'd put my father on a pedestal, I never thought I was very important to him. We were raised in a household where children were meant to be seen, not heard. I think my brothers reacted in very much the same way. Sure, we missed him, and we respected his memory. We maintained the Jewish tradition where no music was played in the house for one year. We weren't allowed to go to the movies either. But there wasn't a deep sorrow.

"The distance we felt was not the result of his travel, but because of the emotional distance he had kept. Married once before, Charlie's first wife had died of cancer at the age of twenty-nine. They'd had two children, Helen and Joe. Three years later, in 1924, he married his secretary Fannie, my mother."

Was she able to compensate for the loss of your father?

"I don't think so. She was never really that attached to us, either. I can remember even as a small kid that she couldn't stand it when we would come up and kiss her good night. Or if we would give her a hug, she would cringe as if we were infected. There was something about her, or in her upbringing somewhere along the line, that made her incapable of displaying affection towards us kids."

Was there any love at all?

"No, there was none visible. She never told us how much
she loved us or what great guys we were. Now, she may have
felt that way. That I don't know. But as a child, I could only go
by what I saw, and what I saw was cold and distant. Maybe that
was common in those days. For a long period of time after my
father died, my mother lost her outward glow. It appeared that
any happiness she'd possessed was removed from her life.
Looking back, I suspect she was probably bitter and only going
through the motions of life.

"We were fortunate that my mother had four brothers and a
sister who lived in town. None of them were married at the time
and they stepped in and helped raise us. To this day, I'm very
thankful for their assistance and companionship. But it also
brought with it a certain dynamic that was not good for my self-
confidence. What evolved was kind of a clan and with it *the
party line*. We were trained not to rock the boat. The party line
was a form of group approval or group acceptance including
how to act, how to think, and who to like. Individualism or
opinions different from the group were discouraged, and we
were kept in line by the fear of being ostracized," Dad
explained.

"I don't blame them. They did the best they could under the
circumstances, but they never really helped us develop any self-
confidence. For example, when we went fishing we weren't
allowed to hold a fishing pole. They were afraid we might lose
the pole—or the fish. I wasn't even allowed to hold the net.
Sorry, they'd say, *you don't touch that*."

Were you angry?

"I don't remember experiencing any anger over it. I just
felt, hey, I guess I'm not really capable of it. I guess I'd

probably lose a salmon if I hooked it. I think my self-esteem was low enough at the time to agree that they were probably right.

"I can remember being affectionately referred to as one of my uncle's *slaves*. Sure, he liked my company. I can even remember one time when he asked me to help him paint the cabin at Green Lake. I held the can. This was typical; not earthshaking or abusive, but looking back I'd have to say it did a job on my self-esteem," Dad reasoned.

"Self-esteem plays an important role in happiness," Dad said. "It's the fabric of your being, the glasses through which you see and interpret the world."

We discussed this subject on a walk taken in late July. It was dawn. The sky was filled with low, gray clouds blunting the morning light. The horizon darkened with each step. It looked like rain. Still, we decided to take our chances. Dad relied on a light windbreaker, and I wore a yellow Marquette sweatshirt and a Red Sox baseball cap, which I had borrowed from Mom's closet.

After a few minutes, we turned the corner onto Grandview Avenue. Bangor High School sat on the hilltop to our left. I was a student there from 1978 to 1981. Not much had changed in the twenty years since.

We walked past the parking lot and approached the school. It was typical of most built during the 1960's, red brick with square aluminum panels that were painted alternately aqua and white.

We passed the auditorium and continued between the softball field and tennis courts, and finally out to the soccer field. We stopped. I remembered soccer practice on fall afternoons. I could feel the excitement of streaking down that field, running with my teammates. I knew the exact spot where I had scored a goal in a victory over Mount Desert Island, one of only a few goals I had scored as a halfback.

Sports had helped me. In my senior year, I was captain of the soccer team. But really it was joining the swim team that built my self-confidence and physical strength. As a sophomore, I could barely swim. By my senior year, I had three top-ten finishes at the State Championship.

Dad was never really into sports. His childhood had been so different than mine.

What was it like during your high school days? I asked.

"My high school days were certainly not as carefree as yours. I attended during World War II, the class of 1945. By the time I graduated, the war in Europe was over and America was fighting Japan in the Pacific. Two of my brothers were in the Navy. One was stationed in the Philippines; the other was preparing for the invasion of Japan. After graduation, I enrolled in Officer Training at Maine Maritime Academy."

Was this the turning point for him? Was this where he became the secure person that I know?

As we walked off the soccer field retracing our steps, I asked my dad if the Service helped him.

"Oh, my gory," he began, "joining the Army made all the difference. You see, the war in Europe was over before I joined Maine Maritime Academy. One month later, we dropped the bomb on Japan, and the war in the Pacific was over. I left the Academy and decided to enlist in the regular Army. When I told my mother what I had done, she said, *Well, that's another fine kick in the pants you've given me."*

Why did she say that?

"She wanted me to be an officer in the Navy, in the Merchant Marines, not just a soldier. At that point, my self-esteem was so low, and this is really true, that before leaving for boot camp I didn't even want to be seen on Main Street. I used to go down side streets to avoid people. I didn't even want them to look at me.

"I was angry and hurt. That's when I decided to sign up for three years instead of the standard eighteen months. I didn't care if I ever came back. But I hadn't reached bottom. The lowest point came in Germany," he said.

"Her name was Eva," Dad continued. "She was beautiful with black hair and crystal blue eyes. She was a Holocaust survivor. We had met at the Council, a place where Jewish GI's and civilian personnel socialized, similar to the USO. We spent hours at the Council just talking to each other, and I fell in love with her. But Eva could not return my feelings."

Maybe she really wasn't that interested in him, I thought to myself.

"I couldn't understand why Eva didn't love me, until she brought me to a party at Ziegenhain. Located about sixty miles outside of Frankfurt, Ziegenhain had served as a prison camp during the war. At this point it was a shelter for over three thousand survivors of the concentration camps.

"As we came over a hill, the camp became visible. It was still surrounded by barbed wire. The gate was open and the old guard tower stood like an imposing sentry. Inside there were rows of long, wooden barracks on brick foundations. The windows all had shutters. Many of the glass panes were broken. There were clotheslines strung on posts and a few small, lifeless trees. The yards were dirt and gravel with some sparse field brush growing wildly. Piles of debris from torn down structures were near the barracks, including some broken cots, likely used for firewood," Dad recalled.

"We proceeded to the party at the recreation center and were greeted at the door by one of Eva's friends. He reached out to shake my hand, his blue tattooed ID number clearly visible on his arm. Most of the people inside looked thin and frail, even though over a year had passed since their liberation. Their clothes were drab and somewhat raggedy."

Were there refreshments? Was there music?

"There was beer. There was wine. But this was not like any other party I'd ever attended," Dad answered. "I had visited several displaced persons camps, so I expected these conditions. What really shook me was what I heard. It wasn't the music. It wasn't the singing. It was that they were all crying and singing through their tears.

"I remember whispering to Eva, *What's going on? They're all crying.*

"Eva did her best to explain. She said, *Happiness is a sickness to us. We don't even know how to be happy anymore.*

"This is when I began to understand. Happiness only reminded them of the depth of their loss. I could see the pain on their faces from the uncounted absence of family, friends, and even strangers. It reminded them of innocent people who'd suffered horribly and died in front of their eyes.

"That's when I knew Eva *couldn't* love me." Dad shrugged his shoulders and shook his head. "Eventually we had to go our separate ways. I felt totally alone. And my pain would still get worse," he said.

"I began to question myself. Having learned that over seventy-five hundred gentiles had been killed trying to hide Jews, I asked myself, *What would I have done? Would I have had the courage to hide someone in my attic at the risk of being executed?*

"I was haunted by these questions and even more haunted by my answer, because I knew I wouldn't have had the guts. My answer was completely inconsistent with my *so-called* ethics. I felt like a coward and a fraud. I couldn't even measure up to my own moral standards. Yet I had the nerve to feel sorry for myself because of Eva. And when I thought of what these people had been through, I felt ashamed.

"That was the lowest point in my life. I was depressed. In fact, I woke up one morning with a headache that lasted for over six months."

Dad was interrupted by a soft rumble of thunder echoing in the distance. Morning thunderstorms are rare in Maine. Yet the dark clouds gathered and the noise grew louder. It was definitely going to rain. By now, we had circled back to Broadway and were looking for a place to stop. Governors, a family restaurant, was the obvious choice. You couldn't miss the sign: a giant caricature of an English governor dressed in a black top hat and formal wear. It happened to be one of our favorite breakfast stops.

We entered the restaurant, walked past the glass dessert counter and waited for the hostess. We were seated at a booth with wooden benches next to a window. Dad kidded with the waitress, asking if she owned the place. This was part of Dad's routine of connecting with people, turning strangers into friends. After Dad finished, our waitress took our order. We hadn't intended on having a full breakfast, so we ordered oversized blueberry muffins and two cups of hot chocolate.

"Would you like your muffins toasted on the griddle with butter?" our waitress asked.

That sounded good to me. Dad shook his head, no thanks.

As the waitress walked to the kitchen with our order, I noticed an electric train circling a track just under the ceiling. The locomotive had several boxcars attached, Bangor and Aroostook Railroad and others. After a few seconds, I focused back on my journey with Dad.

What did you do about your headaches? I asked.

"Ultimately I went to the commissary and spoke to a doctor about them. He informed me that one of the new things being done at the time was electric shock therapy. Remember, this was the 1940s. The doctor did caution me that if I were to use something like that, it was likely I would be a prisoner of needing psychiatrists for the rest of my life.

"The doctor asked me, *How much time do you have left in the Service?* I told him eighteen months. *Great,* he said, *that should give you enough time to deal with your problem.* Then he gave me some advice that I can remember to this day. He said, *You can always go to a psychiatrist. But if you can lick your problem on your own, I promise you that even though you'll have far worse problems than this in the future, none of them will ever seem as bad. You'll have become the master of your problems.*

"This wasn't the battle I'd expected to fight in the Army. When I'd first enlisted, I wasn't feeling good about myself. That was no secret. I joined hoping to find answers to my questions and to perhaps even find myself along the way. I wasn't thinking in terms of my self-esteem. I was just trying to feel comfortable with myself.

"After speaking with this doctor, I realized that it was not just a philosophy of life I was searching for; I was also searching for a psychology of life. I had to become aware of who I was, how I got there, and, finally, what I could do about it. I had to learn what made me tick. This became my new mission," Dad stated. "This introspection is what led to me finding peace of mind."

It happened that quickly? I asked.

"Well, it took me many years to accomplish this. I'm talking about an introspection that forced me to recognize the defining moments in my life and understand the impact of my childhood. I explored questions that determined who I was and how I got there."

What do you mean? I asked, noticing the rain now falling outside.

"Obviously, I needed to examine my life, beginning with my childhood. So I asked myself, what things provided me with a sense of security and what things created feelings of insecurity or inadequacy? What things helped my self-esteem and what things hurt? Anyone in this position should ask themselves:

Were you raised in an environment of
unconditional love?

Was there a lot of emotional support?

Was there financial security or instability?

Did a parent die or was there a divorce?

Did you experience psychological, physical, or sexual abuse?

Was there alcoholism or drug addiction present?

Were you made to feel important or worthless?

Was there sibling rivalry or parental favoritism?

Were you able to develop special talents?

Were your parents perfectionists?"

That's an awful lot of questions, I commented.

"That's just the beginning. I haven't even begun to mention issues such as peer pressure." And then he continued:

"Were you generally accepted or rejected?

Did you walk through life with feelings of confidence or humiliation?

Were you comfortable with your appearance or were you self-conscious?"

I can see why this took years, I said and smiled.

Dad wasn't distracted.

His eyes opened wide, revealing the depth of his belief as he gazed at me. He gently pointed his finger in the air.

"The answers are critical," he said. "They allow you to recognize your needs: acceptance, being right, being perfect, or the need to win. They affect your perception and determine your ability to make decisions, take action, overcome fear, and maintain a positive attitude."

I think I have always taken self-esteem for granted, I said.

"I did, too, up until that point," he replied. "But what I've come to realize is that many people aren't on solid ground. They actually find themselves in a hole. The only question is: how deep? They wake up as young adults, trapped at the bottom, buried alive, and begin the process of digging their way out, one shovel at a time. I'm living proof. That's what happened to me."

The waitress delivered our muffins and drinks.

"Do you have time to pull up a chair and join us?" Dad offered, pointing at the open space next to me in the booth.

She smiled, seemingly amused, and continued about her business.

Dad, I said, you always seem so self-assured. Given your background, how do you explain it?

"I began working on this issue while I was in the Service. One of my assignments was being a clerk in the library. I was able to read a lot of self-help books, including a couple of very important books by Dale Carnegie," Dad explained, *"How to Win Friends and Influence People* and *How to Stop Worrying and Start Living.* Every bit of progress I made was from the books I read. I believed self-esteem could be learned and education became my shovel. That's how I began to dig my way out."

Just by reading?

"It wasn't just reading by itself. My therapy continued with thinking sessions," Dad replied. "When I was off duty, I would go for long walks for hours at a time. I would think and think and think. Generally I would spend more than two hours each day this way. I would review the principles I had learned in the books and give them priority. Then I would track my progress by taking notes. Some days I'd come back with over thirty pages of notes on areas for improvement. At times I'd wonder if I'd ever get to cover them all. Eventually I did," he said with a smile as he buttered his muffin.

"There was another book I read," he continued. "I can't remember the title, but it helped me to understand that it's only human to want to be accepted: I figured I needed to accept myself as well."

So how did you do this?

"By accepting everyone else," he said matter-of-factly. "Anyone who looks in the mirror could witness imperfection, not just me. That's what makes us human. We have strengths and weaknesses. Even the President of the United States makes mistakes. I gave myself the same permission and began to embrace my imperfections.

"With this perspective, I found humor in everyday life. I began to have a deeper appreciation for what I now called life: *The Human Comedy*. I stopped taking everything so seriously. I lightened up. I relaxed and truly embraced others' peculiarities as well as my own. I began to accept myself, to like who I was, and become the secure person you see today."

The skies opened up and it poured. Our conversation was muffled by the driving rain pounding the metal roof of the restaurant. It became difficult to see out the window. Dad took a drink from his hot chocolate and got a bit of whipped cream on the end of his nose. I motioned for him to wipe it off.

You know, Dad, I accept you, even with whipped cream on your nose.

Dad laughed.

It's hard to get a rise out of Dad, I thought. He could handle sarcasm. He could take criticism, even insults. Not just from me, but from everyone. In fact, I don't ever remember seeing him angry. Dad was in a class by himself. I prodded him about handling criticism.

"I can laugh at myself," he answered. "It's probably the best advice I could give anybody. Sure, I might get knocked by criticism or some playful teasing, but it's helpful to be open to feedback. Of course some people project their issues onto others. So it's important to keep things in perspective. But overall, you shouldn't really worry too much about other people's opinions of you. You can spend a lifetime trying to manage other people's opinion of you, but the opinion that matters the most is your own. So do what you feel is right and don't be too concerned about seeking everybody else's approval."

All this from a man who confessed that as a young man he had tremendously low self-esteem.

Did you use arrogance as a way to compensate? I asked.

"Not really," he answered. "The key to self-esteem is being comfortable with yourself and feeling equal to everybody else. Self-esteem is balanced. It's neither inferior nor superior. It's secure, yet humble.

"I can remember when Ike Eisenhower was running for president. His advisers were concerned he wasn't attacking his opponent enough. At one point, I understand Ike said, *When you feel equal to others, neither inferior nor superior, you don't feel the need to attack them.* I think this is what I respected most about him, and it's probably why I voted for him. However, the world is a competitive place and being able to compete is essential. Yet it's important to radiate feelings of equality."

How do you remain humble and self-confident at the same time? I asked.

"By serving my family, my friends and the community and remembering that we are our brother's keeper," he said confidently.

Dad finished his hot chocolate. The toy train overhead made another pass as we asked the waitress for the check. Dad complimented her on her excellent cooking skills, getting one more smile for the road.

The rain eased, and we headed home. Our conversation drifted to lighter subjects. It took another ten minutes or so to return to my parents' apartment. We made a brief stop and organized ourselves for the day and then drove to visit Mom at the hospital.

What about Mom's self-esteem? I asked, making conversation as we passed Governors again, heading back down Broadway towards town.

"I think Rhoda is a very self-confident person. She's never afraid to take on new challenges. She isn't insecure or self-conscious in any way. She doesn't worry about what anybody says or thinks about her. She doesn't care if everybody likes her. She is true to her nature and expects you to accept her as she is," Dad said.

And, you know, that was Mom in a nutshell.

Mom was asleep when we entered her room. Her eyeglasses sat on the nightstand next to her bed. We sat quietly with her. I looked at her lying in that hospital bed. Her head was shaven. There were deep purple bruises next to the stapled incision marks on each side of her head. I breathed deeply to help keep my composure. After a while, her eyes opened slowly. She was awake, though disoriented. She quickly recognized me and gave a tired smile. Even with her limited speech, the first thing she wanted to know was how I was doing, and she was looking for news about her granddaughter Marisa.

She was proud of her family. That was no secret. *We are her legacy,* I thought. I tried not to cry.

And anyone who visited her could see that she was still completely self-assured. She was not the least bit self-conscious, even after brain surgery, lying there bald and bruised. She was comfortable with herself. She knew who she was. She knew her contribution. This was self-confidence.

As for Dad, I had only known him as the secure man who sat beside me. He had dug his way out long before I was born. I was discovering that Dad's security and his ability to maintain a positive attitude set the foundation for having peace of mind.

Walk 3 – A Positive Attitude is a Reservoir

"When I was eight years old my mother took me to the Bangor Public Library. She pointed towards some books and said, You read all the books on that shelf and someday you will be a great man. The shelf was full of Bibles."

This is Dad's recollection of his introduction to both the library and spirituality. It's a story that crosses my mind this crisp spring day in 1997, while I drive to the library to meet him. The windows are down and I hear the roar of the Kenduskeag stream that runs parallel to Valley Avenue. The stream is swollen from the melting snow and is ready for the canoe races that take place each year at about this time. I notice a kayak moving downstream. I hit the accelerator and quickly catch up with him. Within seconds there's only a glimpse of the boat in my rearview mirror.

The great fire of 1911, which devastated most of downtown Bangor, had consumed the original library. People in town galvanized to build a new structure, which opened as the Bangor Public Library in 1913 and is still recognized as one of America's great little libraries. The original building and its replacement were funded from several benefactors in the late 1800s and early 1900s. At the time, Bangor was a major East Coast city and served as one of the world's largest lumber ports. Logs flowed from northern Maine down the Penobscot River to

Bangor and with it the resources to build this library. In recent years, new benefactors like authors Tabitha and Stephen King helped modernize and expand the facility.

With its tall windows and large central dome, the library has a cathedral like quality. I came here often with classmates starting at a young age, as the library is located only a few minutes walk from my old elementary school. We'd descend the steep wooden stairs built into the side of the hill behind the library. This was our gateway to Downtown. On Saturdays it was a great place to hang out before catching a movie at the Bijou Theater.

In front, two winding staircases made of giant slabs of gray granite connect from each side at the central entrance. The portal doors are enormous. They're solid wood, stained dark brown. I twist the brass handle, push open one of the doors, and step inside the dimly lit marble foyer. It takes a few seconds for my eyes to adjust, while I ascend a few stairs polished smooth from nearly a hundred years of wear. The familiar sweet smell of parchment, leather, and wood is in the air as I walk into the main room.

In contrast to the cramped foyer, the main room opens dramatically. Antique cabinets housing the card catalogs and a number of oil portraits frame the room. Above the foyer is another set of marble stairs leading to an atrium directly under the dome. The original reading room to the left is now a reference area. The large brick fireplace and granite hearth sit at the far end of the room. The old children's area on the right is now the computer center. This is the room that leads to the new wing where I'm supposed to meet Dad.

I see Dad seated in the new periodical room next to a large window. He seems comfortable, as he's sort of half reading and half nodding off. Dad could fall asleep anywhere.

I sit in the chair next to him, and he wakens.

"Well hello, Young Fella," he says.

Well, hello there.

Someone recognizes Dad and approaches.

"Hello, Gov'na," this woman says affectionately, as she greets Dad.

"Hello there. Have you met my dad?" He asks as he points to me.

He's used this same corny joke for years when introducing any of his sons.

"No, we've never met."

"Harley, this is Sandy Beach," he says grinning, obviously using his nickname for her. "We work together at Marden's."

"You have quite a dad there. For a guy who only works part-time, he sure makes a real impression on everyone. He's such a character."

That's what people tell me, I reply.

After a minute or so, she leaves.

Do you have nicknames for everyone? I ask.

"Just about."

That reminds me, I tell him, I was in Marden's yesterday and met one of the cashiers. She'd been quietly going about her business, until I mentioned that my dad worked at the store.

"Oh, really," she said. "What's his name?"

Al Bernstein, I answered.

"You're Al's son," she exclaimed. She was beaming. "You tell him that the President of St. Joseph's Hospital said hello."

I'll do that, I told her, as she finished ringing up my sale cheerfully.

So Dad, what was that all about? I ask.

"Well, she's actually a nurse's aide, but I like to refer to her as the President of the hospital," he says simply. "I have nicknames for lots of people who work there."

How did that begin?

"When I first started working there, I felt that there was not enough comaraderie among the staff. So I took it upon myself to try to improve morale, and I did this by creating nicknames. It got to the point where people were coming up to me and asking, What's my nickname? *or,* Why haven't I got a nickname?*"*

How many people work there?

"About forty. It really does wonders for the place," he says, with some satisfaction. "I want to make the people around me feel positive, whether it's people I work with, or a complete stranger working in a supermarket. It's a challenge for me to pick up their attitude. Instead of having a person just filling a bag of groceries for me, somehow I've made a connection, and this person is no longer anonymous. He becomes more interested, like he's serving a friend. It makes the experience so much more personal," he insists.

Is that the payoff?

"Even an anonymous gift creates a sense of satisfaction within the giver," he offers in explanation. "And when I think about it, I must admit any energy that I invest in making a connection or picking up someone else's spirit is actually returned to me. Filling others' reservoirs helps me to fill my own. The feelings are contagious, and they feed and grow upon each other."

Did anyone influence you with this type of behavior?

"I get this from 'The Christophers'—'Light a little candle in someone else's life.' Some people get satisfaction from watching Michael Jordan score a basket. I get the same satisfaction if I brighten someone else's life a little bit, or add a little happiness. To me, it's like scoring a basket. That's why I have this corny sense of humor. It helps me connect with people. That's why I ask store clerks if they own the place, or why I ask a waitress for the recipe for the excellent meal she

just cooked for me. Corny? Yes, but it's harmless and it helps me connect with people. That's what counts."

Is this your secret for dealing with people?

"Maybe. As I said, it's my goal to have a positive experience with everyone I meet. It's not to say that some won't be negative, but I limit the kinds of interactions that lead to negative feelings. I'm very cautious with criticism, putting someone on the defensive, or offering unsolicited advice. Instead, I want to be the kind of person who brings a wave of positive energy. That's the attitude I strive to create within myself. I find it's infectious, and it allows me to inspire others," he asserts.

I don't care if you do fall asleep on company, I tease. From now on, I'm going to call you Mr. Ambassador.

A walk in early August of 2000 brought us to the Essex Street Recreation Area. We hauled our toboggans here each winter in my youth. My brothers and other kids from the neighborhood—Kenny Nyer, Tommy Sensenig and Sue Willey—would pile onto the sturdy maple boards and thin blue pad of our eight-foot toboggan. After a hard push, we flew down the two hundred foot vertical incline, absorbing bumps and the tops of shrubs. There were no brakes. We slid across the frozen bog at the base of the hill. The dried remnants of the prior summer's cattails buckling through the ice slowed us before we reached the edge of the woods. The ride was fast and it was fun! We'd quickly look up to see if anyone had fallen off, searching for lumps in the snow and listening for the laughter. Then we'd brush ourselves off, grab the rope, drag the toboggan back up the hill, and do it again and again into the darkness.

The same old rectangular building where we'd get hot chocolate and take a break from the cold stood at the top of the hill. Grass-covered berms revealed the outline of a skating rink. There were only a few small changes. The parking lot had been extended, which now included a paved basketball court, and a couple of park benches had been added looking out over the hill.

The benches were wet from the morning dew. Dad reached into his pocket and pulled out a white handkerchief. He usually carried two: one for cleaning his eyeglasses, the other for blowing his nose. After he'd finished wiping the benches, we sat down.

A few minutes passed while we sat quietly. I looked down the hill and saw the large open slope leading to the pond and the blue outline of Pleasant Mountain in the distance. *Those were some fun times,* I thought to myself, as I again pictured it covered with snow.

A flock of Canada geese overhead caught Dad's attention. "It's amazing how they fly in formation," he commented, trying to engage me.

I nodded my head and continued to look out over the horizon.

Then we stood up and continued our walk.

Dad asked, "What's on your mind today, Young Fella?"

I took a deep breath and said, this whole situation with Mom has been very difficult for me, as I'm sure it's even harder for you.

"It's been hard on all of us," Dad replied.

I feel like I've fallen through a trap door, yet I'm amazed by your attitude, I said. How are you able to keep such a positive outlook?

Dad thought for a moment, then answered simply, "I have no other alternative. I find that a positive attitude is the foundation for having peace of mind. Reinforced with my faith in God, it's what helps me through tough times like these."

You seem to be doing remarkably well.

"You've got to realize," he cautioned, "a positive attitude is not something you can just turn on when you need it. You can't expect it to be there without effort. For me, it's like a reservoir that needs to be continuously filled. The trick is keeping it full and readily available."

So, how do you do that? I asked.

"It's a habit that I've developed over time. It's a process."

Dad tilted his head and scratched his chin. He looked off into the distance as if referring to a page of notes on the subject stored in his mind. After a few seconds, he turned back towards me and continued.

"It's hard to maintain a positive attitude, like trying to hold water in your hands," he said, clasping his hands together and forming a bowl to illustrate the point. "The conviction of my beliefs determines whether my reservoir is rock solid or fragile like glass."

It sounds like it's all in your mind, I observed.

"That's right," he stated without hesitation. "I've chosen to live in a world where God exists. And I'm practical. I've chosen to believe in a world where there is purpose and meaning in my life. I can see no benefit to living in a godless world or living a life that has no purpose. Why would I bother?"

Dad stopped, closed his eyes for a moment, and rubbed his forehead up and down with his fingers.

As if thinking out loud, he said, "This is the core of my spiritual beliefs, to be constructive and do my full and fair part at all times. These beliefs along with a good sense of humor, help me maintain a positive attitude. Like the biblical character David, a positive attitude can help you conquer any Goliath. A lot of the process I use was developed right here."

He pointed at our old house as we rounded the corner.

What process are you talking about?

"Maintaining a positive attitude," Dad said. "Mine started by monitoring it. I became determined to be its guardian. I decided to fill it only with the positive and refused to let it be poisoned by other people."

You're making it sound easy again, I said, lightheartedly.

"Then let me try again, because I don't want to oversimplify this. It's no easy task. It's taken me many years," Dad responded. "You see, each morning I pre-program my attitude for the day. It's a warm-up session that primes the pump. It starts with personal prayers, then recitation of some spiritual affirmations.

"A spiritual affirmation is a stated belief—something I want to accomplish—which I'll say out loud with full enthusiasm. This is where I affirm my positive attitude, my belief and commitment."

Do you have an example?

Dad recited his mantra, which, among other things, included role models such as Mahatma Gandhi, Martin Luther King, Jr., and Nelson Mandela. It ended with him asking himself to choose between the positive and the negative.

Dad said, "My answer is consistent every time: I choose the totally positive, optimistic, enthusiastic, constructive, creative, decisive, confident and open-minded team."

I could tell he had recited it hundreds—if not thousands—of times over the years. Even more telling was the calmness in Dad's expression when he had finished. His confidence was contagious.

I asked Dad about how he had selected each of these role models.

Dad replied, "Martin Luther King represents courage and conviction; Nelson Mandela represents a living example of these same characteristics; and Mahatma Gandhi is the ideal.

"But don't get hung up on my choices. If you're interested in this form of affirmation, use role models that represent the character traits most important to you. It's really a personal preference. You might choose Mother Teresa, Tiger Woods, Oprah Winfrey, or Guy Lombardo. It's up to you. Most importantly, you must understand—like each of my role models must have understood—that the results of your life will be either the reward or the consequence of your attitude. So be in charge. Don't let the tail wag the dog," he instructed.

Did you have a morning session today?

"I have a session every morning."

Did it work?

"What do you, mean, *did it work*?"

I don't know, I said. Did it improve your attitude?

"With me, it's more of the maintenance of an attitude that is already positive," he explained. "Over time it's become automatic. I don't even have to think about it anymore. It's like breathing, or my heart beating."

Are there any shortcuts?

"There may be one—smiling. I quickly learned that the best way to protect my own attitude from negative influences was to become a positive influence on others, and the simplest thing I can do is smile. It not only warms me up, it's contagious.

"In fact, my morning sessions end with something I call *Smiling Contemplation.* It's my own form of meditation. I begin by getting into a relaxed position. The best place for me is in my recliner. I sit back and put a big smile on my face. Then my reservoir takes over and floods creative feelings back into my mind. I feel like I can tap into the positive waves of the universe and find it quite inspiring."

Dad continued to explain that it's easy to maintain a positive attitude when things are going your way, but the skill that so many people are searching for is the ability to stay positive even when things turn against you.

"To do it, you've got to be resilient and prepare, like the boxer who trains to keep moving forward even while receiving blows," Dad said. "Another thing is prevention. We can't eliminate all the negative from the world, but we're free to promote the most constructive thoughts and feelings. Our challenge is to meet the negatives head on."

When did all of this start for you? I asked.

"I'm not exactly sure. But I remember years ago—I'm talking about when I first got out of the Service—I was a troublemaker. This was when I worked for Uncle Nate at his produce store."

You, a troublemaker?

"Well, I used to talk about Nate behind his back with some of the guys who worked there. I'd say that Nate was cheap and that Uncle John was a jerk. Anyway, I found that with my bad attitude it was easy to commiserate with others, and we fed off each other's negativity.

"Of course, you know, when I was a kid, my uncles— including Nate—stepped in and helped provide for us. So here I was, bad-mouthing one of the people who'd supported me as a kid. That's when I realized, wait a minute, this is wrong. I work for my uncle, he pays my salary, and he's always been good to me. If I don't like working for him, or I don't like the things he does, then I should leave and not work there. Otherwise, it isn't right to talk behind his back. This was the point where I began to take control of my attitude."

By this time, Dad and I headed back up Broadway for the last leg of our walk. I returned to the discussion about one of Dad's role models.

I don't understand your connection to Guy Lombardo, I said.

"In my day, Guy Lombardo and his Royal Canadian Orchestra were quite popular. They were known to play *the sweetest music this side of heaven*. I took Rhoda to see Guy Lombardo on our first date."

I raised my eyebrows.

"You might find this amusing," he said. "When Rhoda and I went on our honeymoon in New York City, Guy Lombardo was in town, coincidentally. He was playing at the *Roosevelt Grill*, and we went to hear him. During a break, I went up to him and said, *You know, you played Cupid for us*, referring to the fact that he had played during our first date. He didn't respond, and I could tell that Guy Lombardo was *totally unimpressed*. But that didn't change my attitude about him, one bit."

Walk 4 – Never Pull the Plug

What was the toughest decision you've ever had to make? I ask Dad on a walk taken before Mom's second cancer diagnosis.

Dad pauses for a moment.

"I'm not really sure. Okay, I've got it," he says after a moment. "It was deciding to marry Rhoda, to spend the rest of my life with her. You see, about two years after I returned from the Service, I got engaged to Rhoda. Asking her to marry me was easy. It happened on our fourth date. Ours was a whirlwind romance. The hard part came a month after our engagement. Out of the blue, I received a letter from that gal, Eva. You know, the girl I had flipped for, over in Germany."

Oh yeah, I acknowledge.

"She wrote and told me that she was finally ready. She now thought she could experience love again, and hoped I was still interested. And, get this: she was living in Montreal, no less, the same city as Rhoda."

So what did you do?

"When I got the letter, I was confused and, at the same time, excited about the prospect of seeing her. In fact, I broke off the engagement with Rhoda for about a week."

Oh, you're kidding!

"No. It's the truth. When I got that letter from Eva, I decided I was going after her. Once I had a few days to think about it, I changed my mind. I wasn't going to chase after the past. I loved Rhoda and knew that she was my future."

How did you reach that conclusion?

"I was attracted to Rhoda and up-in-the-clouds in love with her, but I think it was a guilty conscience that made the difference. I figured, how could I do something like that? I had already asked Rhoda to marry me. It simply wasn't fair to her. I couldn't hurt her like that. And I have never once regretted it."

What did you say to Eva?

"I had only received her letter and I hadn't spoken with her. So I wrote her back and explained that I was in love with Rhoda and that I had moved on. That was the last I heard from her," he said.

You're lucky Mom took you back.

"Yes, we're all fortunate, or you guys wouldn't have been born! She was visiting her Aunt Jean in Bangor at the time and I went to see her. She was quite gracious about the whole thing. Somehow she understood, and that was the last of it."

Making decisions can be hard at times, but it's strange to me how often people struggle with this, I said. What should I do? They ask. Or what would you do? The anxiety is apparent, even from things that seem fairly trivial.

"You're right. Making decisions can be stressful. Indecision and uncertainty create doubt, which in turn causes

the anxiety that interrupts a peaceful mind. It's not that it's always simple. On the contrary, it requires effort and a system. The payoff I get is the confidence l have in the decisions I make.

"It doesn't guarantee that every decision I make will be perfect," he insists. "Far from it. Mistakes should be expected and understood to be part of the process. What I find is that many people live in fear of making mistakes and are therefore unwilling to make decisions.

"But I ask, what's wrong with making mistakes? The only thing to be concerned about is not repeating them. Heck, even Thomas Edison made mistakes. In fact, I understand that he discovered over 10,000 ways how not to make a light bulb! Clearly, Edison looked at life as a learning experience. Why shouldn't we? I generally believe it's better to make a poor decision that can be corrected than none at all.

"Of course, when it's crucial, I'm a lot more careful. The decisions that I spend the most time with are the ones that will affect the rest of my life—the ones made at the edge of the precipice. Like my decision to marry Rhoda.

"It's not that everyday decisions shouldn't be considered thoughtfully, as well. I just don't see the need to get too wrapped-up in being perfect. When I make a mistake, it only reminds me that I'm human. I keep it in perspective. Life is full of decisions; some will be bad, but I'll bet more will be good. What I've found is that the freedom to make mistakes grants me the freedom to make decisions."

What's your system? I ask.

"Well, for simple items, I try to make decisions quickly. I don't want my mind cluttered. I find that indecision can become a habit.

"As for serious issues, the first thing I do is separate my feelings from my dealings. When facing any problem, I try to size up my emotions. Emotion can cloud my judgment and often runs contrary to my goals."

Dad looks me straight in the eye, points his finger, and with full conviction says, "It all begins with honesty. How honest are you with yourself? Do you live in a world of denial? Can you objectively and open-mindedly look at yourself and admit your own fears and insecurities?

"Look, people can be selfish." He pauses, then asks, "Are you willing to identify motives in yourself that are not considered good; for example, greed, anger, jealousy, vanity or pride? Can you recognize your need to control a situation or your desire for perfection? The answers can help you understand what's driving you. This is what I consider first, before making any decision," he says confidently. "Then I can begin to address the issue at hand."

How do you handle things when they're serious?

"The best advice I can give you is to have a set of values that allows you to do the right thing. That's what I always try to do. At the same time, be slow to judge or condemn other people's choices until you've walked a mile in their shoes.

"I refer to these values as Moral Tools. They're sort of like a compass to help you navigate.

"The first is Constructiveness," he continues. *"Are your motives or actions constructive or destructive? Are they positive or negative, helpful or hurtful? Having a constructive direction in life is absolutely necessary.*

"Once you've determined that you're being constructive, the next step is to examine whether it's fair. Like the decision I made with Rhoda, it really all came down to a sense of fairness. I try to live my life under the rules of Fair Give and Take. It's not that you're required to give all the time—nobody should. On the other hand, no one should take more than his or her fair share, either."

This seems more like an art than a science.

"That's right, but kindness has its own reward. It comes from the heart and shouldn't be considered an obligation. Yet there is another side to giving that includes responsibility; namely, being your brother's keeper. This is where you're responsible for helping others, whether they are family, friend, stranger, or foe. There is a duty beyond basic fairness that's required and makes up the third part of the Moral Tools. I call it The Golden Rule of Insist: do unto others as you insist they do unto you. This is the minimum standard of fair treatment that I expect of myself.

"Finally, I feel the need for a holistic approach. This is where I balance the Spiritual and the Material. I think the first time I used this as part of my decision-making process was just after I graduated from college, in the early days of my marriage. I believed the stock market was the place I could make big money. I was considering spending my full time on it. What I found was that I got so absorbed in the material challenge that I lost all spirituality. I wasn't able to keep it all

in balance. I had to choose one, and I favored spirituality. So I dumped the idea of the stock market and ended up in sales.

"I believed it was okay to focus only on the material so long as things are going your way. But when you're in trouble or looking for purpose in your life, that's where the spiritual becomes important. As for the monks up there on a mountaintop living exclusively in the spiritual world, they too can lose hold of a lot of life's meaning. The challenge is to keep it all in balance."

What if there's a conflict?

"When there's a conflict," Dad states, "I recommend the spiritual every time. For me, it's the final judge."

There was one decision Dad would not make alone. This decision could require Dad to spend the rest of his life without Mom.

In late August of 2000, Mom was moved to Ross Manor, a nursing home, to continue her therapy. Her speech remained impaired, and her physical condition had deteriorated to the point where it was even hard for her to get into a wheelchair.

I was aware that the radiation treatments hadn't worked. I knew that the surgeries, considered aggressive, had removed her tumors and most everything else that I knew as Mom. What I didn't know—or refused to believe—was that Mom was terminal.

While in Virginia I depended upon others for information. The news I was getting wasn't good. Mom had to be placed on a feeding tube because swallowing had become increasingly difficult for her. Worse still, she had pulled the tube out on several occasions.

I sat in my office early one September morning and waited for a conference call with Dad and my brothers to discuss whether or not to reinsert Mom's feeding tube. The room was dark, but grew lighter as dawn approached. The ticking clock and some birds outside my window kept me company.

I imagined Dad's calm voice from one of our walks and closed my eyes. I began to review the task at hand and how we were going to make our decision. I prayed for help.

The phone rang and jarred me back to the present.

We reviewed the facts. Prior surgery had prevented Mom from having a feeding tube connected directly to her stomach, so it had to go down her throat. We were also advised that in her condition she was likely to choke if she kept trying to pull it out. Without it, she could starve, as spoon-feeding had become nearly impossible.

The most troubling issue was Mom's unequivocal statement, repeated many times over the years: *Never pull the plug*. Yet her recent actions were in direct contradiction. She had pulled out her feeding tube several times, knowing she couldn't live without it. She had even vocalized something I never would have believed she could say, *I can't stand living like this*. When I heard it, I was shocked. She had always been so strong, such a fighter.

These were the facts. There was no disagreement. Neither option—to reinsert the tube, now that it was out, or to leave it out—was acceptable. Mom's only hope seemed to be a miracle.

What should we do?

It appeared that my brothers and Dad were resigned to leaving her feeding tube out. They had been on the front line with Mom and had witnessed her steady decline. I was removed from Mom's daily suffering since I lived hundreds of miles away. I didn't think I had the right to even offer my opinion, especially when it might not be in harmony with theirs. But they insisted that I state my position, and that it was only fair to share in the burden of making this choice.

We had done our best to separate our emotions from the decision at hand. Our discussion had been centered on what was in Mom's best interest. We explored all possible courses of action, as we had done in the past. As one would expect, the toughest part was answering the moral questions: What was the constructive thing to do under the circumstances? Was it fair? If we were in Rhoda's position, what would we want or insist upon? Most importantly, what was the correct spiritual thing to do?

Had it been me, I wouldn't have agreed with Mom's desire to *never pull the plug*. I wouldn't have wanted that course of action for myself. However, I was willing to honor her wishes. But what were they? It seemed Mom had made a new decision about her life and possible death. I was confused. I wasn't sure of her intentions, especially not being as close to the situation as the others.

We all recognized Mom's brave fight. How could we give up? But what we had to determine was whether Mom had given up. Dad had already made up his mind. He was willing to let go; so were my brothers. But I wanted the feeding tube put back.

There we were, our emotions in check as we tried to objectively consider her future. Dad had also decided that if there were any doubt, we'd hang on as long as we could. My choice communicated that doubt. Dad and my brothers respected my concern and we decided to give it another try. Still, a line had to be drawn, as we were likely to be in this position again. We needed to make a second decision should she intentionally pull it out again. We all agreed that if this happened again, we would leave it in God's hands.

We had made a tough decision thoughtfully, morally, and without guilt, though not without pain. I am confident we had done everything in our power to save her and I'm sure Mom would have approved of how our family faced the issue of her mortality.

As it turned out, she pulled out her feeding tube the very next day. This time we honored her wish and left it out. I was at peace with this decision. But that peace would not last long.

Walk 5 – Permission to be Human

As Mom's situation worsened, tensions grew. Rick and Heather tried desperately to feed her, coaxing every sip. Dad was focused on Mom's suffering and was concerned about prolonging the inevitable. They were equally concerned about Mom, but they were pulling in different directions.

Rick's actions created feelings of guilt inside Dad, as Rick subtly, or not so subtly, challenged Dad's compassion for Mom. Dad wondered silently, or perhaps not so silently, how prolonging Mom's suffering was compassionate.

Rick is three years older than me. We were close enough in age to be rivals at times; yet being older, he'd often fought my battles for me on the playground. Now he was fighting a far more difficult battle, one for Mom's life.

Rick mobilized family and friends to sit with Mom around the clock. He even considered bringing her home with him and hiring private nurses. Dad, on the other hand, began distancing himself. He visited Mom several times a day, but spent less time with her. He did his part by contacting the nurses and ensuring Mom got as much of their attention as possible.

Dad would ask me, *Why does Rick want to do this?* Rick was just as mystified by Dad's behavior and wondered, *Why not?* I ignored them both, hoping the issues between them would vanish, and they did, until my next visit.

Kari, Marisa, and I departed on the United Express shuttle just before sunset. The sky was a brilliant red and the clouds reflected gray, blue, and lavender. I thought about Mom's life and the decision we'd made regarding her recent care.

Bud picked us up at the airport in Portland. It was late, so we stayed overnight at his house before heading up to Bangor. Bud and I are close, even though he's eight years older. I've always looked up to him. He's the brother who let me stay overnight at his college fraternity when I was only thirteen.

Early the next morning we drove the two and a half hours to Bangor, exiting the highway at Broadway and stopping at the traffic light near Tri-City Pizza. I called Dad on my cell phone to let him know we were now only a couple of minutes away.

We went straight to Ross Manor. Built ten years ago, the building is a sprawling one-story structure housing fifty patients. It's located right around the corner from my parents' apartment, which was convenient for Dad. Bud dropped us off at the front entrance and continued down the street to pick up Dad.

There was a large birdcage on a table near the front desk. The flutter of the parakeets brought the place to life. Several patients in wheelchairs were admiring the birds and chatting with each other.

The nurse at the desk directed us to Room 201, down the corridor to our left, past the chapel. The room was full of "Get Well" cards, which adorned the walls, and family pictures were everywhere. Easy listening music was quietly playing on a radio in the background.

Mom's nurse was feeding her something that the menu identified as chowder. It did not look the least bit appetizing to me. I said hello, catching Mom's eye. She raised her eyebrows, nodded her head, and smiled. She turned her head and motioned the nurse to stop. I sat down in the chair across from her.

As the nurse got up to leave, she let us know that Mom had only taken a few sips of dinner and asked if we could try to get Mom to eat a little more. I knew that Mom had been losing ground, even with the feeding tube. Now no matter how hard everyone tried, she was barely eating.

Mom's eyes were tired. She seemed sad, resigned to her fate. *These were the same eyes I had stared into as a child that were so reassuring.* I pictured an emergency room visit when I was ten years old. I had fallen on a broken glass bottle and she watched as I'd received twenty stitches in my calf, having been given only a local anesthetic. I begged her to cover my eyes so I didn't have to see what was happening. She withstood my screams and through it all her presence helped me. And now, these many years later, it was my turn. What could I do for her?

She looked frail, having lost a lot of weight over the past few months. Her hair was gone. The bruises on her head from the surgeries had faded a little and, with them, her spirit.

How are you doing? I asked.

"So-so," she nodded slowly, groggy from the pain medication. Mom recognized Marisa and motioned for her to come closer. A tear formed in the corner of Mom's eye and rolled down her cheek. She whispered the word "beautiful." Marisa gave her a hug. Then Marisa sat next to Kari at the end of the bed. I tried to encourage Mom to have some more soup. Reluctantly, she took another tiny sip. A few minutes later she was asleep.

I left her room and headed toward the nurses' station. Dad and Bud were in the hallway. Bud continued on to visit with Mom, but Dad remained behind to talk with me. He was clearly upset. Dad's attitude had changed since Mom was moved to Ross Manor. He used to be so confident that Mom would recover, but now he was acting like he knew that Mom was going to die. What I had been ignoring from back in Virginia was becoming immediately clear: Dad was overwhelmed. So much, in fact, that he jumped all over me.

"You know," he said forcefully, "Rhoda's physical therapy has become too painful for her to continue. Her therapists have told me for some time now that she isn't getting any better; same with the nurses. One of her doctors said she wouldn't have done half the things that Rhoda had done, even if it were for the doctor's own mother.

"Her speech therapist was so concerned by her refusal to eat that she warned, *If you won't eat, you won't live.* Rhoda told her she didn't want to live anymore; she'd given up. The nurses have the same impression, and I'm also convinced she's given up. So I don't understand why he's doing this," Dad said sternly, his tone unfamiliarly hostile, his face red.

I knew he was referring to Rick's efforts.

Dad had never seemed so agitated. He was lecturing me, talking at me.

Why is he trying to convince me that Mom's going to die? I thought. *Why is he rubbing salt in my wound?*

What's your point? I snapped,

The question silenced him. It silenced me as well. I could tell by his expression that he hadn't been aware of the impact of his actions or how repetitious his words had been. He took a moment to consider my question, but I couldn't deal with it just then. I turned around and headed back to Mom's room to collect myself and join the others.

Here was a man who seldom—if ever—lost his self-control. I can only remember him losing his temper one time in over thirty years. Now he'd been acting so defensively.

What made him lash out like this?

The answer was obvious. The confrontation between Dad and Rick could no longer be ignored, nor could the reality of losing Mom.

After twenty minutes or so, I stepped out and again went down to the nurses' station to find Dad. As expected, he was busy entertaining them. When Dad was done, I asked him if he'd join me for a walk. He was ready to go and anxious to discuss what had just happened. We headed towards Husson College.

We walked the campus loop road in silence and avoided others. This was new territory for our walks. Today my teacher seemed far off course from the many lessons he'd given me over the years. He wasn't listening to Rick's point of view. He couldn't admit he'd made a mistake, and he wasn't recognizing his own emotions.

We needed to discuss what had happened earlier. Though I eased into it by asking him if he considered himself a good teacher.

"I'm okay. The best teachers are humble, like Gandhi, and have mastered the art of patience and self-control. They're comfortable with what they know—and with what they don't know. And, at the same time, their motives are pure. As for me, I consider myself merely a good listener."

There's no better listener than Dad. He's patient and usually so self-controlled.

I don't get it. You've never acted this way. I know you're upset about Mom, but what else is going on?

"You know," he said softly, "sometimes I think you may know me better than I know myself. When you asked, *What's your point?,* it forced me to ask myself, Why am I acting this way?"

I felt a little guilty and said, You don't have to explain anything to me. Considering everything you're dealing with, you have every right to be upset. Besides, some of these things may be just too personal to share.

Dad began to explain anyway.

"I never told any of you this, but when Rhoda moved to Ross Manor, I happened to find a piece of paper on the floor that said she'd been admitted as a "terminal" patient. The nurses told me right from the beginning that they would do everything they could to help keep her comfortable. *We never give up,* they'd said. But it was clearly communicated that they were not expecting her to recover.

"She was placed in a room with the shades drawn and the lights out. Your brothers, on the other hand, immediately opened the shades, turned on the lights, and had me bring in a radio to break the silence. They hadn't given up.

"What I realized was I didn't have the ability to help Rhoda the way they were helping her. I felt guilty because I wasn't contributing and doing my full part.

"After her surgery, I was hopeful and was with her at the hospital almost around-the-clock while she received her treatments. Now, in her present condition, I visit her only three times a day. It's hard to sit all day and witness the woman I'd spent fifty years of my life with, raised my children with, deteriorate right in front of my eyes."

It was rare for Dad to demonstrate human frailties. In such an instance, I'd tease him by saying, *That was mighty human of you,* reminding him and, more importantly, reminding myself that he was human like the rest of us.

This was one of those times.

"There's no question in my mind as to what the problem is," he said, in a serious tone. "I'm being defensive and rationalizing that I'm giving her the best care possible. I'm going to all the nurses and making sure they're doing everything they can for her. But as for personal care," he cleared his throat and continued, "I'm not giving it to her."

Why do you think you're dealing with it this way?

"I'm not sure. I guess I'm trying to avoid my feelings. She's dying and maybe I'm not prepared. Perhaps I'm trying to shut out my grief. This could be the result from my childhood when my father had died. I don't know.

"What I do know is that here are Rick and Heather doing this great thing of organizing people to be with Rhoda, include-ing having Heather's mother and their friends stay with Rhoda, each person for an hour and a half at a time. And I'm refusing to participate. Now that's really a powerful thing. I've refused to take my turn. I just can't handle it. I'm fighting the battle of dealing with Rhoda's death, and I think I just want to shut it out of my mind."

Then I recited one of my teacher's many lessons on accepting your own limitations: *When challenged by others, the test is to fully understand their position. When you're wrong, admit your mistakes. When you're right, refuse to accept the burden of proof by defending yourself.*

Dad's face relaxed. He rubbed his chin and grinned. I could tell he recognized his own words and they were helping him.

"That's what I've been doing: I'm lashing out at my own guilt," he said after a long pause.

"No matter what happens, I usually say, hey, I did the best I could. I admit my mistakes and compensate those who may have been hurt. I've learned far more over the years from my failures than my successes. This time I'm way off track," he admitted.

"You know," Dad said, "I recently discussed the subject of guilt with Bud, and I could only remember a few instances where I'd actually felt guilt. One time was when Bud was a baby. I remember yelling at Rhoda during an argument in front of him, and it made him cry. That was the last time I ever argued with Rhoda in front of you kids. Then there was the time I'd criticized Bud at the dinner table and ruined his meal. That was the last time I criticized someone at the dinner table or in front of others. Finally, there was the time I spanked you without giving you the chance to explain yourself. That was probably the last time I ever did that. Since then, I always make sure to understand a person's position before criticizing.

"But I can see, in this case, I haven't done that with Rick. Here I am attacking him for what he's doing. I've even got you rattled," he said, patting me on the shoulder. "I don't feel good about the way I've handled things."

You know, Dad, here I've judged you. We all know that Mom doesn't want to live like this and that she's going to die. I just didn't want to be reminded of it by anyone—not even you.

That's just how I've chosen to deal with it, I continued. Each of us is processing this differently. Rick may have the need for a vigil and wants to make sure he's tried every effort to make Mom comfortable. You may need to start the process of becoming detached, preparing yourself for the future. Either reaction is understandable.

In my opinion, you should give yourself *permission to be human.*

You just need to step back from this for a minute and remember your own advice: *embrace your imperfections.* Then cut yourself some slack and accept how you're dealing with this. It's not easy, and there's no right way. If you're going to judge your own actions, it's okay by me. If you determine you want to change how you're handling things, that's okay too. But avoid judging yourself against how others are reacting.

"You're right," he said. "The issue for me is not to lash out and attack what others are doing. That's only a defense mechanism. Instead, I should worry about my own actions."

You know, your contact with the nurses has really helped Mom. They're treating her like a friend. What more could be asked?

A few days after this visit, I received a call from Dad and heard the familiar, "Well hello, Young Fella.

"I wanted to let you know that I was grateful for our conversation the other day. I'm glad you were honest with me about how I was dealing with Rhoda and all. I want you to know that it served an important lesson for me. In fact, I'm convinced that it led me to having a conversation with her today.

"This afternoon I received a strong feeling that I needed to go up and see Rhoda. So I dropped what I was doing and went up the street to Ross Manor. When I entered Rhoda's room, she just stared at me. She didn't even seem to recognize me.

"I said, Rhoda, do you know who I am? She just stared at me, motionless, with a blank, somewhat puzzled look. Rhoda, I repeated, this is Al. Do you know who I am? Still there was no answer. All right, Rhoda. You always said to me and to the boys that if you ever became seriously ill—even if you went into a coma—don't ever pull the plug. Instead, come and talk to me and I will hear you. So today I'm going to talk to you.

"I reviewed fifty good years of marriage and finally said, you know, Rhoda, there are over five billion people in this world and a little over half of them are women. But there is not one woman that I would rather have been married to for the past fifty years than you. We were not perfect. Of course, there was never a question about our loyalty to each other. But I was not always the best companion. Often, I got lost in my writing, and for that I truly apologize.

"Rhoda continued to stare at me as if I were a stranger. But she also reached for my hand and squeezed it slowly, three times.

"And, you know, Rhoda, you were not always perfect, either. To put it mildly, at times you were more than a bit of a controller. She continued to stare blankly at me, but she grabbed my hand again and squeezed it three more times.

"At this point all I could say was, I love you. In response, she again squeezed my hand three times. Then I held her hand for another ten minutes until she closed her eyes and fell asleep.

"I walked out of the room with tears in my eyes. You see, over the years it has been Rhoda's tradition that whenever I said, I love you, she would reach for my hand and squeeze it three times representing the words *I—Love—You*. The feeling I got was that Rhoda understood we were there for her and that we had honored her wishes. Her message to me was that life is precious until the very end. It was comforting, yet I knew this would be our last conversation in this world.

"I relay this story to you in appreciation for our recent talk where you straightened me out. Those three little words, *What's your point*, helped me to regain my composure. I believe it's what allowed me to receive the intuitive flash that led to my last conversation with Rhoda."

As it turned out, appreciation would be my next lesson.

Walk 6 – Appreciation of a Thousand Little Things

I thought I'd seen my mother for the last time. Somehow she held on, and two weeks later I returned.

Bud picked me up at the airport. By this time, he was driving from Portland at least once a week to visit Mom. It was Thursday evening and traffic was light. During the ride I thought about my parents. They had spent most of their adult lives in the small town of Bangor, Maine. They hadn't set the world on fire, weren't world leaders, not even local leaders. But underneath there was so much to think about.

We arrived in Bangor around nine o'clock and went directly to Ross Manor. Bud had prepared me for what to expect, so I wasn't surprised to see how gaunt she looked. Her eyes were open, but fixed. She wasn't aware of much.

I sat with Mom for a while. I held her hand and told her I was there. Her breathing was very strained and heavy. She'd take a breath, pause for several seconds, then struggle for another. I tried to comfort her, or maybe myself, by telling her it was all right and that everything was going to be okay.

Bud made a brief stop at Dad's and then returned with him. I stepped outside the room and spoke with Dad in one of the sitting rooms. He told me that he was glad I could be with Mom again. Then we talked about Mom's struggle.

This has been very hard, I said.

Dad nodded in agreement.

"Rhoda's initial diagnosis was a tremendous shock, but I was convinced she would beat this thing. Then, probably the worst day of my life, they found a brain tumor. That's when I began to realize it might beat her," he said with resignation.

"I think the saddest day occurred three weeks ago. Rhoda sat with us outside in the private courtyard, in a wheelchair. It was a beautiful September day, sunny and warm. You could tell by her expression how much she was enjoying the afternoon. Such a simple pleasure, one which most of us take for granted. Even when it got a little chilly she still wanted to stay outside. That was the last time she got out of bed."

We sat together quietly before returning to Mom's room. After a while, Bud took Dad home for the night. I stayed with Mom and wanted to give her permission to stop fighting, wishing she could just let go and be free from her agonizing battle. Before leaving, I silently prayed, *Please take her. Surely, she doesn't need to suffer like this any longer.*

The next morning we returned. Mom was still hanging on and didn't appear to be experiencing any pain. Nothing could be done for her and we made sure not to leave her alone.

She was now laboring for breath. Her chest moved slowly as she struggled to draw in a breath, stopping for as much as ten to twenty seconds at a time. Then she'd gasp and the air rushed into her lungs.

You can let go, Mom. Your job is done here. Don't worry about us; we'll always be there for one another.

Dad joined us because he knew it was time. We shared stories about Mom, celebrating her life and her uniqueness.

Instead of sadness, the atmosphere was one of warmth, love, and even laughter.

"I always felt that her love for us was unconditional," Bud said. "To this day, I can't figure out who's her favorite. I also don't understand why the grandkids can jump around on the sofa, bring a dog into the house, and eat as much chocolate as they like. Can you imagine if we'd tried to do that?"

We all laughed. Mom did have a way of spoiling her grandchildren.

"She always put family first," Rick said, shaking his head sadly, "even while undergoing cancer treatments."

"She rarely went to bed before 2:00 a.m. While we slept, she'd prepare a batch of kasha and bows because she knew how much we loved it. Then she'd call the airlines to make travel arrangements for another family reunion," Bud said.

Heather reminded us that, "Rhoda's name was known to many people at United and Delta Airlines."

You know Mom was one of the first people to put financial pressure on the airlines with her late night calls to different supervisors, maneuvering schedules until she got her price, I added.

"Mom always knew how to make a little money go a long way," Rick stated. "The local grocery store managers were very familiar with Rhoda. If the scanned price came up wrong, she'd request her refund plus whatever incentive they offered at the time."

I remembered Mom being so excited the time she bought two huge boxes of cereal. I think they were Corn Flakes. After the sale price, double coupons, and the further discount she got for a scanning error, the price was only a dollar a box. It was as if she'd won the lottery.

"To her she had won the lottery," Bud said. "With the money she saved, she could afford to drop some cards in the mail to her grandkids, buy Hershey bars for the children at Beth Abraham, or maybe even donate a few bucks to the Ronald McDonald House. Mom appreciated the little things, and that's what made her life rewarding."

Dad was listening but not participating. I tried to draw him into the conversation and asked, Hey Dad, do you remember that time when Mom went out of town and you got in trouble for eating the wrong meal on the wrong day?

"Oh yeah, I remember that very clearly. She had prepared three dinners for me and with them, a schedule directing me to eat a specific meal on a specific day. But I decided to have the stuffed cabbage on the first night contrary to Rhoda's schedule. When she came back, for whatever reason, I told her. Then she paused for a moment and looked at me and said, *I'm not going to cook for you anymore if you can't follow simple instructions.*"

There was laughter.

Bud jumped in to her rescue. "Mom always applied herself to something with great discipline and excellence. That's a lesson that has served us really well."

Dad looked at me curiously as I mentioned Bangor's best-known citizen.

Stephen King had stopped at the Maine Coat Town one afternoon while Mom was working there. This was not unusual as he came in from time to time and Mom liked to wait on him. As he approached her with his purchases, he asked if she'd take a personal check as his credit cards were at home. Without missing a beat, she replied, *I'd be happy to take a check provided you can show appropriate identification.*

Dad smiled.

I looked out the window from Mom's bedside to see a brilliant sunset. We continued with our stories about Mom's passion for life and family as the light outside her window began to fade. Leafless trees formed shadowy silhouettes in the dusk. And when the sun set for the day, it also set on Mom.

Mom was able to let go of her life in our presence, surrounded by the people who loved her. It was quiet, it was peaceful, and I was thankful. There were tears for our loss; but what I remember most were the expressions of appreciation we had for the life she'd lived, the life she'd shared with us, and the peace we knew she deserved.

She passed away on Friday, the 13th of October, 2000. On most Fridays, Mom would light candles to welcome our Sabbath. There would be no candles on that night.

We took some time with Mom before she was taken to the funeral home. An hour or so later, Mom's bed was empty, stripped to the blue industrial mattress and steel frame. There was nothing more for us to do, so we packed up Mom's personal items into paper bags: the "Race for the Cure" baseball cap she'd worn to cover her baldness, the "Get Well" cards, teddy bears, her bathrobe and eyeglasses.

After we'd finished we stepped outside. It was a crisp autumn evening, lit by a full harvest moon. We could see steam from our breath as we consoled each other in the parking lot.

That full moon also signaled the start of the ancient holiday of Sukkot, the commemoration of the Jews wandering in the desert. At that moment, we were alone and lost without her.

We huddled for a little while. Then, Dad, Bud and I returned to the apartment to make phone calls and begin funeral arrangements, and Rick and Heather went home to their boys.

We stayed up late that night. Dad was in reasonable control. He reached Mom's brother, Warren, and a few of her closest friends.

The next morning, Dad was already awake when I went into his room to check on him. He was lying on his back over the covers in his underclothes. The fingers of his hands were interlocked and placed comfortably on his stomach. He was whispering with his eyes closed.

How are you doing? I asked.

"As good as could be expected."

I heard you whispering to yourself. Are you okay?

"I'm all right. I'm just saying my prayers."

If you don't mind me asking, Dad, what prayers are you saying today?

"It's the same prayer I've been saying for years, most mornings when I get up. It's a personal prayer of appreciation."

Is it written down?

Then he reached into his nightstand and pulled out a folded piece of paper. "I know it by heart, but from time to time I refer to it. And when it gets worn out, I rewrite it on a fresh sheet of paper. You can read it," he said, handing it to me.

I glanced at it quickly. It began: *In deep appreciation for my spiritual attunement and the wonderful and inspiring blessings that you have given me, including the blessing of awakening each day.*

After I finished reading the entire page, I said, that's quite a prayer.

"I've always believed that the path to adjustment begins with appreciation," he stated. "In fact, those affirmations are what I believe my life is all about. They confirm my purpose and meaning in life."

I usually assumed that Dad would want to take a morning walk with me, but today I asked. Are you up for a walk?

Without hesitation he said, "Yes, but give me a few minutes to get ready."

We both quietly went about getting dressed so as not to disturb Bud, who we thought was still sleeping. As I tiptoed past the pullout couch, Bud quietly acknowledged my presence.

Dad and I are going to take a walk; do you want to come along?

I generally didn't invite anyone to join our early morning walks. I looked at these walks as our personal time. But today I asked Bud to join us because I didn't want him to be alone.

We followed the standard route, passing the high school and then on to our old neighborhood. Suddenly, I heard a familiar rumble as Rick pulled up in his long-running gray Le Baron. He parked it quickly and jogged up to us. He said he'd gone to Dad's and found no one there. So he figured he'd find us out here.

We were at the corner of Essex and Lancaster, our old home. With Rick falling naturally into stride, we turned left and headed towards the recreation area where we'd gone tobogganing as kids. We stopped at the benches overlooking the hill and wiped off the melting frost with our hands before sitting down.

Dad was unusually quiet. His eyes were bloodshot as he scanned the horizon. He sat rigidly with his right hand squeezing his left, trying to maintain control of himself. We each took turns relaying appreciation for a thousand little things about Mom in an effort to console Dad, each other, and ourselves.

Bud shared a letter he'd written Mom earlier in the summer, which he'd found in her papers. He pulled it out of his pocket. It seemed to capture her essence.

It discussed her devotion to family, which was something Bud expressed as "her great legacy that we should embrace." And he continued, "Your love is unbounded, unqualified, and even-handed. You champion our every cause. And the joys of your life—your grandchildren—know that you treasure them every day," he read with some difficulty.

Rick's sentiments were very much in concert with Bud's. He recalled how Mom had endured the steroids, radiation treatments, surgeries and chemotherapy, focusing on one thing: beating cancer so she could get more time with her family.

"Yet she never complained," he said.

Rick considered the past two years since Mom's original diagnosis as a gift. He was grateful for the time he got to spend with her at barbecues, going to Bar Harbor, and watching her play with his children, Josh and Adam.

Bud also reminded us how, throughout her life, Mom never cut off family or friends, and never burned bridges. "A family argument or a disagreement with a friend may seem really significant at the moment, but be completely unremarkable with the passage of time. This was Mom's gift to us."

Normally, when the four of us get together our conversations are quite animated. We're all good communicators, except we interrupt each other and tease each other a bit. On this day, however, the conversation was subdued. There was no vying for the stage.

Throughout our discussion, Dad mostly nodded his head in agreement or stared off into the distance. I could tell he was in pain. Still, I asked him how he was doing.

"Oh, hanging in there."

So what's on your mind? I pressed.

"Mostly, I'm counting my blessings. I had fifty good years with Rhoda and for that I'm thankful. Maybe it's selfish of me to have expected more, especially when you think about the miracle of existence: It's a wonder any of us even get the opportunity to be here at all. And I'm really fortunate to have you three boys," he said with assurance.

Still, I couldn't stop myself from worrying about Dad, who no longer had his organizer, his companion and, most of all, his caretaker. Dad had always referred to Mom as his benevolent dictator who helped him stay organized. I wondered how Dad was going to manage without her.

Walk 7 – Leaves in the Wind

"Did I ever tell you about an unusual dinner I had with Mom and Dad in Italy?" Bud asked, as we drove to Mom's hometown of Montreal for her funeral.

"We were in Florence, in this wonderful little restaurant in a cobblestone alley across from Dante's birthplace. It was an intimate place, more for the locals, and no one spoke English. Mom was getting a little frustrated by the difficulty in communicating. Each time our waiter would come back to our table, Mom would raise her voice. I turned to her and said, *Volume doesn't help with the translation.*

"For the first course, we were directed to a round table in the middle of the room, which was covered with exotic appetizers. Then came the main course, and I enjoyed every bite of veal scallopini. I think Mom and Dad had the same dish. I could see they were satisfied, but not thrilled. So I asked if they enjoyed the meal. And in a voice that everyone could hear, Mom said, *Well, it's no Olive Garden!*"

Stories like this helped pass the time as we traveled from Bangor to Montreal. Kari, Bud and I rode together in a car with Dad. Rick, Heather Josh, and Adam, were in their van, along with Marisa. The seven-hour drive took us through the mountains of Maine, New Hampshire, and Vermont. We had traveled these roads many times as kids. Today's trip was not so carefree, but was just as memorable.

Do you remember each summer the five of us would pile into the car and head out to Montreal? I asked Bud. Remember the bumpy back roads and that diner where we got those greasy hamburgers and french fries? We looked forward to those trips months in advance. And somehow, Dad would manage to get lost each time. I think we turned around in the same dentist's driveway several times over the years. Remember that time you begged to get out of the car and walk to Montreal because you were carsick?

"How could I forget? With all the hideous almond-flavored Dramamine we took, to this day I still can't come within fifty yards of an open bottle of Amaretto," Bud replied.

"Of course, it was the ride itself that was the problem," Bud reminded me. "For a long time, I had thought that we'd just had weak constitutions. It wasn't until much later that I realized it was Dad's driving. He couldn't seem to keep a constant speed; accelerating and braking his way through the mountains."

This time I was driving. It was a warm October day, without a cloud in the sky. The leaves were at peak color and changed with every turn in the road and different angle of the sun, from red to orange to golden yellow—right through till sunset.

The changing season was a message that gently illustrated the cycle of life, transforming what could have been an unbearable drive into something beautiful. I wished Mom could have seen it. And for whatever reason, I felt she had.

We stopped at the Balsams Resort in Dixville Notch, New Hampshire, to take a break. There was nothing else around for miles. In the 1920s it had been a gambling joint. Today, it's a grand hotel and ski area. The town is best known as the first town in America to vote in each Presidential election. They get up just after midnight on Election Day and vote in antique wooden voting booths that are kept in the basement of the hotel.

As we were strolling back to our cars, a couple of bright red maple leaves swirled past us in the breeze. Bud picked them up and tucked them into his shirt pocket.

The ride through the notches was my favorite part of the drive. Over the years, we had seen eagles, bears and moose nearby, but there were no discoveries today. We arrived in Montreal just after dark.

The memorial service was held the next morning. Rick spoke first and shared his thoughts about Mom.

"I want to tell you the story of a famous painter, Renoir, who had crippling arthritis for the last few years of his life. Every brush stroke was extremely painful. Yet he created one of his greatest masterpieces just two years before his death. One day a friend, who was watching Renoir as he continued to paint through agonizing pain, asked, *How can you keep painting?* Renoir replied, *The pain will pass—the beauty remains!* This is the message that I hold onto when thinking of Mom's last days. I pray our pain will pass, but the beauty of her life will remain with us forever."

Heather read the eulogy Bud had prepared and my cousin Judah said a few words on my behalf. What struck me was the appreciation we all felt for Mom. The words spoke of her passion for excellence in everything she undertook and, most of all, her love of family.

After the service we continued directly to the cemetery for the burial. Unlike the sunlit day before, this day was cold and gray. As I stepped outside, I felt raindrops lightly tap my cheeks. Someone offered that the raindrops were angels' tears for my mother.

If you've ever been to a Jewish burial, you'd remember it. If nothing else, you're forced to accept the reality of the situation. First, there's the smell of fresh dirt piled high by the grave. Then you watch the casket as it is gradually lowered into the ground. The sounds are penetrating. You hear the solemn *Mourner's Prayer,* a song of appreciation. But it's another sound, like no other on earth, that signals the finality of it all—the sound of that first shovel full of dirt striking the casket with a desolate thud.

It's considered an honor for the immediate family and other close friends to assist with the burial by shoveling dirt onto the casket. Dad was first. Bud, the oldest son, went next. He reached into his pocket and pulled out the crimson leaves he'd found the day before, releasing them with some soil into the grave. Rick followed Bud, and I, being the youngest child, went next.

Looking down, I remember feeling too young to be losing my mother. I felt cheated—not for myself as much as for Marisa. Mom would never see her bat mitzvah, her college graduation, or her wedding.

After the funeral we went back to Uncle Warren's apartment for a catered reception. Mom's family came from all over the United States and Canada to be with us to honor her that day. Mom, like her mother, had been a catalyst for our family and had helped keep the extended family close.

After everybody had left, I got the chance to catch up with Dad. From all outward appearances, he seemed okay. But I needed to check.

How are you holding up?

"I'm not sure. I feel kind of numb. Maybe it's a defense mechanism kicking in. I don't know. I probably won't know until this whirl of activity calms down, after all the people leave, and I find myself alone, back in my apartment in Maine," he said softly.

Then he changed the subject.

"You know, before Mom's original diagnosis of breast cancer, probably about two and a half years ago, I had been having intuitive feelings that Rhoda was going to get seriously ill in the coming year and that she ultimately wasn't going to make it. After having had such premonitions, dealing with her breast cancer and witnessing her decline over the past three months, you would think I'd have been better prepared for this day."

How could anyone have prepared for this? I asked.

Dad shrugged his shoulders. We sat quietly in our chairs, not needing to speak. We were helped simply by each other's presence. But I knew that in the future this would not be the case. At some point the absence of Rhoda, his companion for fifty years, would take its toll.

I promised myself that I'd call him every day for one year. I thought it would ease his loneliness and give me the chance to see how he was dealing with things.

November 2000: *Why do bad things happen?*

"Well hello, Young Fella," Dad said, making use of his Caller ID. "What's on your mind tonight?"

It's amazing what's going on with the election, I said, referring to the 2000 Presidential race. I don't like what's happening. It's unsettling, I said.

"I don't like the way either party is handling things, but politics is a dirty business," Dad stated.

Were you an election supervisor this year?

"No, Rhoda never signed us up and without her, I didn't feel like doing it myself. Besides, I only worked the polls as a favor to Rhoda. When she became the precinct warden, she begged me to help her and be her assistant. So I figured it was part of being a good companion, and I joined her. She was up on all the rules and I didn't know as much as she did. But somehow, psychologically, she felt if I were there, I could back her up if there was a problem.

"The really colorful part was that I don't think I helped her that much. I just spent time kidding around with some of the folks that came in to vote. I'd say, *You can't vote in this election, you've got to be eighteen.* The other poll workers always looked forward to me coming there. Rhoda used to tolerate it. Somehow I wonder, is it possible that she may have liked some of my corny sense of humor and even enjoyed playing the straight man?"

I don't know, I answered. I think she needed you there, and your sense of humor was part of the deal.

"You're probably right," Dad admitted.

You know, I've been thinking about Mom's battle with cancer, and I'm having a hard time understanding all the suffering she had to endure. What's your take on why bad things happen?

He thought for a moment, then addressed my question with another question: "How can anyone answer one of life's unanswerable questions?" He let that hang in the air momentarily, then continued. "That's why faith is so important. Believing that God has a bigger plan than we can understand answers the question, *Why do bad things happen?* What I've done to address this issue is to paint a picture, consistent with my religious beliefs, which serves me best. I've not only chosen to believe it, but also to train myself to believe it.

"Mainly, I've come to believe that we do not live in a Garden of Eden. Obtaining things freely, without effort, would rob us of much of life's satisfaction and opportunity to grow. With this, I also accept that life will bring its share of good and bad. I recognize that no one is above it—including myself—and everyone should expect a full share of the negative as well as the positive. I certainly don't rejoice over the negative, but I do accept the fact that bad things must happen.

"Are you still awake, Young Fella?" Dad asked, suddenly.

You haven't lost me yet, I answered.

"For me," Dad said, "I believe everything that happens serves a purpose, whether or not it is easily understood. We need the challenges in order to give life purpose: pain to appreciate pleasure and failure to appreciate success.

"Of course, nobody really knows God's plan, and that's probably a good thing. I think it limits the anxiety that would be created by knowing about the pain to come. And at the same time, we're not robbed of the thrill of life's many successes.

"You might consider this a rationalization. But a constructive rationalization is likely to bring peace of mind. In my opinion, the answers to life's unanswerable questions are less important than your ability to deal with the questions themselves. Ultimately, finding an acceptable answer—or being comfortable with no answer at all—is better than the mental anguish of an unending search."

December 2000: Accepting loss

"Well hello, Young Fella. What's on your mind tonight?"

It's strange that we still don't know who's going to be our next President. How bizarre. And, you know, I don't believe all those people in Florida really voted for Bucchanan. What do you think? I asked.

"I don't know, but did I ever tell you that we had the same problem with this style ballot in Maine once? It was about thirty years ago. It was the kind of ballot where you pushed down through a punch card. Things didn't quite line up. It was very confusing. I couldn't tell who I was voting for. The next election the process changed, and there hasn't been a problem since. But with what went on in Florida this year, I only hope they get it right," he said.

So let me ask you, I echoed, changing the subject, what's on your mind these days?

"You know, I've come to realize that Rhoda was not someone I owned, but someone that God loaned me for fifty years. And for that, I'm thankful.

"In fact, one of the hardest lessons I've had to learn from this experience is that you can never fully prepare for loneliness. You can never fully prepare for pain. These are things I first had to feel before I could adjust to them."

You seem to have accepted Mom's death.

"Basically. I can find no benefit gained from denial. I had no choice but to accept her passing, and that's what I've done."

January 2001: Keeping a positive attitude

"Well hello, Young Fella," Dad answered on cue. "What's on your mind tonight?"

I want to know how you keep such a positive outlook.

"Oh, there's no secret," he answered right away. "I actively work on my attitude each morning through spiritual affirmations and prayers of appreciation."

You still do that every day?

"Oh, absolutely," he said firmly. "However, every day isn't completely accurate. You know, there could have been days where time didn't permit it, or a time during a depressed moment when I skipped some things. But I try to keep it going consistently. It's how I continue to fill my reservoir, even during the toughest times.

"It takes a lot of energy to grieve, and it draws on my reservoir. By the evening I'm worn down. I'm tired physically, mentally, and spiritually. I need rest for my body and mind and replenishment of my spirit. So when I get up each morning I try to fill my reservoir. It's a habit that makes God my partner."

Dad then reminded me of the continued need for faith.

"I think we talked about faith not too long ago—or has it been a few weeks? In any case, the biggest risk when things go wrong is losing faith. At this point in my life, when things go wrong it's not a reason to lose faith. I have a strong belief system. So when negative things happen, I have the ability to take the good with the bad. It's part of the Cosmic Pattern. Everybody gets a turn."

Did you ever lose faith after Mom died—even for one day?

"No. Not even for a moment," he said, without hesitation. "Now, I'm not dogmatic, nor do I think I've got all the answers about God. For instance, I don't claim to know who or what God is. Though I do see God as a creative force, and I've never lost faith. I've accepted my loss of Rhoda as I accept that someday I'm going to leave this world as well. Sure, I feel pain and continue to grieve. But I accept death as an inevitable and natural part of life."

I'll tell you something that I've almost lost faith in, I said.

"What's that?"

Our electoral system. And I'm glad that all that election business is over, I said.

"Me too," Dad agreed. "Hey, that reminds me. I bumped into Jill Weber the other day. I think you know her. She used to work the polls with Rhoda and me. Really, she was Rhoda's assistant, even though I had the title. It turns out that she's taken Rhoda's place. I warned her that I'm not showing up to work at the next election. *Sorry,* she said. *Rhoda is not going to allow me to let you off the hook. You're working the polls as long as I'm running it. I did your job all those years. Now you're going to help me!*

"She had me there. I must have had a guilty conscience, so I agreed.

"You know," Dad continued, "I think the election results were wrong. But maybe having George Bush as President was meant to be."

February 2001: Being angry with God

"Well hello, Young Fella. What's on your mind tonight?"

I've been wondering, were you ever angry with God?

There was a long silence. Finally, he stated, "When we lost Rhoda, I honestly don't remember having a thought that resembled anger. I just had to accept it. I understood that Rhoda had to pass away, as everybody's turn comes. Sometimes people might question why God acts in certain ways. But how can you get angry with someone or something that has given us such a beautiful world?

"What I recall most is my wish that it would have been me instead of Rhoda. Selfishly, I would rather have gone first and not have had to experience the pain. But the pain was grief, not anger. Some people might get angry, but they'd have to find a way to release that anger to regain their peace of mind."

But what about parents who lose a child? I asked. Don't they have the right to be angry?

"Oh, absolutely. Losing a child would probably be one of the hardest things to accept in life."

It seems so unnatural, I said. The elderly are expected to pass away, while children are supposed to grow up and shape the world.

"The death of a child does not violate the Cosmic Pattern," Dad responded. "It does break what we consider to be the normal human cycle. But that expectation is a human desire, and the Cosmic Pattern ignores our desires. You know, my brother, Bob, and his wife, Dottie, lost one of their twin daughters, Carly, when she was only six years old."

Weren't they angry?

"Yes. They were absolutely devastated. And this is something we've discussed over the years. Bob admitted to me that he had been very bitter and angry at the world—perhaps for two years, maybe longer. He related to me that he was even resentful of other people's good fortune. Not that he'd wished anything terrible on anybody, but there was no room for joy in his life—for himself or for anyone else.

"Bob told me that the first year was really tough. In fact, you were born a few months after this had happened. I remember inviting Bob and Dottie to Bangor to attend your naming ceremony. At the time, I told them that a happy occasion might be good for them. But they couldn't come. They were still in too much pain.

"A few years later, Bob told me he had been really hurt from that conversation. In fact, he said he was very much annoyed with me at the time. From what I remember, Bob had expressed his anger and had wondered how anyone could even talk of happiness when they were going through such tragedy. He said something to the effect that, *Our loss is so profound, we can't even begin to think of happiness*. At the time, he didn't think they'd ever be happy again.

"Without having suffered in this way, I had no idea of the depth of his pain. I've told you before that when our father, Charles, died, there was basically no mourning. We kept wishing and hoping that he could come back. But we never went through a period of deep mourning. As you know, his disappearance was never even completely discussed with us kids. This was the example that had been set, and so I wasn't in touch with what Bob was going through. I don't know if that's a good explanation, but that's how I was raised."

I don't think I could have handled it, I admitted. How did they get through it?

"Bob and Dottie were fortunate—they had each other. As I understand it, they talked and talked about what had happened. An awful lot of couples that experience this kind of a tragedy see their marriages fall apart. But that wasn't the case for them. They grew stronger—not weaker—and drew even closer in their marriage. They were each other's therapists. And that was lucky for them, because in those days there wasn't group therapy or grief counseling like there is today. So they suffered together and helped each other through it.

"Another thing that really helped them was that they were able to talk with Dottie's parents. You see, her brother had been killed back in World War II during The Battle of the Bulge. And like most people who lose someone, her parents were crushed, but ultimately survived it and healed. Being able to talk to them was helpful.

"Bob was also very close with his father-in-law and thought of him as his real father. I will never forget one conversation with Bob where he shared with me his father-in-law's views on pain and acceptance. He compared the pain of losing a child to the inferno that lifts a rocket into space: Instantly there is intense pain; yet over time, it keeps moving farther and farther away. The pain that had started with the intensity of the sun becomes more like the glimmer of a distant star.

"The thing of it is, people can accept and in time adjust to life's most painful moments, just as Bob was able to adjust. Today, Bob and Dottie are happy people. They enjoy life, are content where they are, and are appreciative of their blessings. They have a good marriage, beautiful children and grand-children, and feel as if they couldn't ask for more.

"Recently Bob told me, *We may even appreciate the things we have even more, having suffered the way we did.* Even so, he reminded me that they would never fully get over it. They still look at pictures of Carly to this day, wishing she were here with them. It's a scar that will never completely disappear.

"This is not out of the ordinary," Dad offered sympa-thetically. "I read an interview with Ike Eisenhower in *Reader's Digest.* It was given when he was seventy years old. It discussed the fact that the eldest of Ike's two sons died at the age of two. It was something that he claimed affected him his whole life. So Bob and Dottie are in pretty good company.

"Bob did have one regret, however. Due to his grief at the time of Carly's death, he hadn't talked with his kids enough about it. He realized years later that just as our mother had never talked with us about the disappearance of our father, he too was unable to talk to his own children about the loss of their sister.

"Perhaps, like Bob, my mother just didn't have the strength to discuss it. But talking is such a vital therapy. You've got to talk about loss and let the inner pain work its way out. In my case, I think I've done this with you three guys."

March 2001: Forgiveness

"Well hello, Young Fella. What's on your mind tonight?"

You know, in all our discussions about anger or resentment, you haven't mentioned anything about forgiveness.

"Well," he said. "I think forgiveness is the ability to accept loss and let go of anger. For me, forgiveness is essential for having peace of mind. This applies to any resentment or hostility, not just in the case of accepting the death of someone you love.

"We often carry the burden to forgive someone who has hurt us. And such forgiveness is advisable, whether the hurt was caused intentionally or unintentionally. The key for me is remorse. If a person who has hurt me is remorseful and tries to make up for what they've done, I feel the need to forgive them. It's that simple. It's important to relieve others of their guilt, just as I want to be relieved of my guilt after making amends when I hurt someone."

So how do you forgive someone that has done something horrible to you or to someone you love?

"I don't know. Some things require God's forgiveness. I hope I would try understanding, and maybe this would help me let go of my anger.

"When experiencing a loss, why should I punish myself by harboring resentment? Anger is punishment. It's a poison that crowds out the good things. Martin Luther King, Jr., at the historic March on Washington, cautioned, *Let us not seek to satisfy our thirst for freedom by drinking from the cup of bitterness and hatred.* He knew that people who are angry inflict far more punishment on themselves than on the object of their anger.

"By the way, did I ever tell you that I participated in several marches in Bangor during the early 1960s? Of course,

I was a strong believer in civil rights. In fact, one time I spoke at a rally in the park next to the library. The speech was given from a platform located right next to the statue of the three lumbermen. I believe the rally was organized in protest of what George Wallace was doing in Alabama as he continued to block African-Americans from entering the public schools."

Really, I said. Were there many people there?

"Probably about a hundred people, mostly white, because there were only a few African-American families in town at the time. I think the Talbots were there, and the Leaks and the Dymonds. You know I worked with Bob Talbot at Viner Music. He ran the service department. His brother Gerry was the first African-American elected to the State Legislature."

Do you remember what you said in your speech?

"No. I can't recall. It was so long ago. But I do remember receiving some hate mail from one guy. His language was so angry. I didn't even respond. I felt there was nothing I could say to a man living with that kind of hatred."

What about revenge? I asked.

"I don't believe in revenge. It's destructive. Revenge only creates unnecessary hate and hostility. Sure, negative people and negative conditions must be dealt with firmly and fairly. I believe in seeking justice. For example, putting someone in prison is not revenge—it's fair. It's fair to keep someone off the street in order to prevent others from being hurt.

"But, you know, you don't have to seek revenge. People punish themselves. Dishonest people are not happy. They're tormented. They become victims of their own lies. They spend their lives constantly looking behind their backs. How peaceful is that? So, no, I don't seek revenge. I don't want to become a victim of my own resentment."

Dad was making progress as demonstrated in our conversations. What began with appreciation evolved into his acceptance of Mom's death. Yet full adjustment would require more time. A major setback was only one phone call away.

Walk 8 – Calling all Cars

It's 7 a.m., the morning after Halloween 1998. Kari, Marisa and I are in Florida. We're renting a house about ten miles from Disney World.

The early morning twilight creeps in through the blinds. It's quiet, except for the ticking of a clock and the hum of the refrigerator. A loud pounding on the front door breaks the silence.

We don't know anyone here. Nobody should be knocking at our door, especially at this hour.

I pull back the blinds to see a squad car from the Sheriff's Department parked in front of the house and an officer in a dark uniform standing on the front porch.

Is somebody hurt? My heart beats a little faster. I open the door and ask, Is there a problem, officer?

He says, "No, not really. But do any of you know a Rhonda?"

I nod yes, recognizing his mistake.

"Well, call her," he says. "She's very worried about you."

Considering that we stayed out until one o'clock in the morning, enjoying Disney's Halloween Parade, I realized the concern. Mom must have been calling us all night, wondering where we were. Darn that Caller-ID, that must be how she got our phone number down here.

After I finish speaking with her and calming her down, Dad gets on the phone.

Were you worried, too? I ask.

"Are you kidding?" he answers. "I slept through the whole thing."

The telephone rang one quiet Sunday morning in June of 2001. I scrambled down the stairs, hoping to catch the call before the next ring, not wanting to wake Kari or Marisa. It was Rick calling to tell me that Dad was in the hospital.

I'm not ready for this, thinking the worst, as I sat down at the kitchen table and braced myself for the news.

Rick told me that Dad was having some chest pains and trouble breathing. The initial report suggested congestive heart failure, likely a complication from Dad's prolonged high blood pressure. Rick gave me the number to Dad's room at Eastern Maine Medical Center so I could speak with him.

It seemed like only yesterday that Mom had been admitted there, though it had been almost a year. My thoughts turned to the many calls I'd made to Mom during her illness. We'd just talk about the simple events of an ordinary day, avoiding more pointed questions such as, was she afraid?

Mom was a very private person and this question just seemed too personal. Eventually, I did broach the issue in an email. But by then it was too late. She didn't have the strength to answer. She may not even have read it. And on the day she left for the hospital, which turned out to be our last real conversation, the words just wouldn't come out.

Not wanting to make the same mistake with Dad, I went into my study and called him. I wished we could have just taken one of our walks.

My hands were shaking while dialing the number. I took a deep breath and tried to calm down. As the phone rang, I pictured Dad alone, in a sterile hospital room, wearing his gold-rimmed glasses and a hospital gown.

Will he even answer?

After a while, he picked up the phone and said weakly, "Hello?"

Hi Dad, it's Harley, I said softly.

"Well hello, Young Fella."

How are you doing?

"I'm doing okay," he said, with a light cough that grew more intense.

What are you hearing from the doctors?

"They're looking into the possibility of congestive heart failure."

Then he reviewed the events that had brought him to the hospital: chest pain, shortness of breath, swelling in his legs.

Not wasting any time, I asked him if he was worried.

"Worried? Nah. I don't believe in worrying. I don't worry about anything until I have a genuine reason to worry. I hope I'm not worrying you."

Incredible, I thought, *he's not worried.* Dad had always taught me that it was perfectly natural to worry. I could imagine his voice, *Concern is helpful; it forces you to deal with your problems,* he would say. *But don't lose confidence in the future. Don't create a void that's too easily filled with worry because, in my opinion, worry paralyzes your thinking. It's the enemy of a peaceful mind.*

Those were his instructions. *Was that Dad's secret?*
I wondered. *Was that what made him so unique? He never worried?*

Can you remember a time when you were scared? I asked.

He thought for a while and answered, "Probably the time
you were kidnapped; that's the one time I really got shook."

Dad often talks about an incident from my childhood as the
time I was "kidnapped." I was eight years old and a friend had
invited me to join his family on a summer vacation to Boston
and Plymouth Rock. We returned more than a day later than
expected. They never even called my parents to say they would
be late. And none of their friends in Bangor knew where they
were. When they finally brought me home, it was almost
midnight. Mom and Dad both cried.

"Your mother spoke to more police officers in more states
than most mothers, but there's no law against it," Dad said,
adding a little levity. "That time Rhoda probably called every
police department in New England looking for you. She was
frantic. Through most of our marriage, I let Rhoda do the
worrying for both of us, but on this one occasion, I was every
bit as worried.

"You know, she probably called the police more than a
dozen times looking for me over the years. In our early days
together, I remember her calling the police when I was an hour
late coming home from a class at Boston University. She called
the Boston Police Department and the officer on the phone
asked her, *Does he drink? Does he run around? No*, she replied
to each. *Then relax, he'll be home soon*, the officer correctly
predicted."

Dad's calm demeanor was infectious and I began to breathe a little easier. He continued to fill me in on the details of his situation, the tests that were scheduled for the next day. He didn't seem the least bit upset.

While Dad spoke, I glanced at an old photograph sitting on the bookcase in my study. It was a picture of Dad taken with his brothers when he was a little boy on Blackstone Street in Bangor. Seldon, his older brother, was wearing a white sailor suit with navy blue trim. Dad and his twin brother Bob were dressed in white and appeared like Raphael's *Two Angels*, with their curly reddish-brown locks.

Were you worried when your father disappeared?

"No. I'm sure I've told you this before, but I just wasn't worried."

You don't seem too worried right now either.

"I've been through worse than this," Dad added, as he retold the story of how he had survived a fall down an elevator shaft.

"It happened when I worked at Viner Music Company, back in 1965. I'd been on vacation. While I was gone, there had been some problems with the elevator. On my first day back I came in early, before anyone could tell me about it. Most of the lights in the building were out, but I was in a hurry to get the replacement stock out of inventory and down to the showroom before the store opened. So, in a rush, I went to grab the elevator. Viner Music had the manual kind where you slide the door open yourself. With no sign warning me of any danger, I slid the door open, stepped inside, and down I went—two floors to the basement.

"On the way down a voice came to me, as clear as your voice is today, saying, *Relax, everything is going to be all right.* So I relaxed. Along the way, something caught my pants, tore them, and slowed my fall. I landed on my head, hitting the cement 20 feet below. *Wham!* In that moment, I knew what it was like to get knocked out by Mohammed Ali. I struggled to my feet and, of course, some of my co-workers came to help me.

"They had either heard me hit the ground or heard me yelling. They ran downstairs and broke the door open. I was bleeding out of the back of my head and didn't realize how badly I'd been hurt. They called an ambulance. I told Ben Viner, the owner, that I would see him later that afternoon. Well, I was out for a month. They took X-rays, but there were no broken bones, not even a concussion. In fact, on my medical records it said, *Suspected Concussion*, so in case something developed later on, they could confirm it.

"When Rhoda asked the doctor, *How serious is it?* He answered, *Take a raw egg and drop it on the floor; that's what happened to your husband's head.* Rhoda was really upset and tried to get more information. But in response to her pointed questions, he snapped, *What do you think I am, a Philadelphia lawyer?*

"When Rhoda saw my doctor again—this was while I was still in the hospital—she broke down and cried. Then she said, *You know, if it were your wife, you would be pretty upset about this thing too,* or words to that effect. The next day, he called her and apologized, up one side and down the other.

"And when I went in to get my stitches pulled out, you crawled into his desk and started ripping through his papers and throwing them all over the floor. You were probably eighteen months old at the time, and Rhoda said to the doctor, *I'll get this straightened out.* But he said, *No. Let him do what he wants to do.* I guess he felt guilty."

So, Dad, how come this didn't turn into your lottery ticket? I joked.

"It was my lottery ticket. I survived, didn't I?"

I mean, it seems to me you could have sued and got a lot of money. Did you ever talk to a lawyer about this?

"Well, when I got out of the hospital, I went downtown and bumped into an acquaintance of mine who was an estate attorney. He said, *Get yourself the best lawyer you can. I know someone who got hurt like you and wound up with a brain tumor many years later.*"

Were you worried about this happening to you?

"No, I wasn't a bit concerned. I felt, right from the beginning, that everything was going to be all right.

"When I got back to work, the Viners wanted to talk to me. They said, *Hire yourself a good lawyer.*

"*Look,* I said, *I got no kicks. It was an accident. I don't want to sue you guys.*

"That's when Sam Viner said, *You've got to protect yourself. Don't worry about suing us, we've got insurance— you're suing the insurance company.* He even recommended an attorney.

"So I went to that attorney, one of the best in town, and learned that I could collect worker's compensation from their insurance company. I couldn't sue my employer for negligence. Instead, we had to sue the elevator company.

"As the attorney prepared me to go to court, he asked me several questions: *Were the lights on? Was there a warning sign? Did it appear that the elevator was there when you opened the door?*

"I told the truth. The attorney was annoyed. *Come on now,* he said, *that's not the kind of answers we want to get from you.*

"Then, I asked him, Don't we swear to tell the truth, the whole truth, and nothing but the truth? *Where did you get that idea?* he retorted. *That's what you see on television.* It reminded me of why I dropped out of law school," Dad said.

"So the night before I went to court, I prayed very hard. I said, *look, I only want to win if I am entitled to win.*"

I don't follow you here, I interrupted. Were you worried you were going to lie?

"No. I knew I would tell the truth. I was praying that the judge would make the right decision and not be unduly influenced by my personal situation. I didn't want him to make an emotional decision just because I had a wife and three kids. You see, I believed I had been negligent too. True, there was a faulty elevator and there should have been a sign warning people, but I should have turned the lights on and checked to see if the elevator was there before stepping in. I was rushing and wasn't thinking.

"When everything was over at the trial, the judge who was handling the case ruled in favor of the elevator manufacturer. He determined the Viners could have done more to prevent the situation and I should have been more careful as well. However, he said, *I want to go on the record as saying that this is one of the rare times when we heard a witness who was totally honest.*

"And that's my story," Dad said, simply.

A nurse came into his room to check on him.

"Hold on a second," he said. Then he warned me that it might be a minute or two.

I could hear him kidding around with her: "Maybe I should be the one taking your blood; the results would be better."

While Dad was preoccupied, I thought about some discussions we'd had about Mom. Over the past few months, Dad and I realized that none of us had ever talked with Mom about her fears. That was taboo. Her method for dealing with fear, rightly or wrongly, was denial. And we accepted that.

Mom was a worrier—but not for herself. She was concerned mostly about others. As for doctors, Mom was petrified. She was a sickly child, having a goiter operation and a misdiagnosed appendicitis that nearly killed her. As for routine physicals, besides when Mom was pregnant, she never had them. Mom would get so annoyed with Dad's prodding her to see a doctor, that he finally gave up trying.

When Mom first discovered that she had breast cancer, she waited until after a family vacation to tell us about her problem. Evidently, she had never had a mammogram until she discovered that lump. I didn't know that I was supposed to ask my sixty-six year old mother if she'd ever had a mammogram. Still, I felt guilty.

When the nurse finished with Dad I asked him, Was there ever a time you thought you were going to die?

"A couple of times. But the time I came closest to death was when I had gastritis. I'd been greedy. I was working overtime during the Christmas rush—making big money, skipping meals, coming in early, staying late, not taking lunch, not even taking coffee breaks. Nothing. I was running around like mad and ended up with something I thought was the flu.

"After a few days, Rhoda noticed that I was very pale and that my fingernails had turned white. Dr. Meltzer checked me out and took a blood test. Internal bleeding was suspected, and he told me to get up to the hospital quick.

"I drove myself to the hospital, and they gave me four pints of blood. I was in trouble. They admitted me for some tests. Then, in the middle of the night, a nurse woke me up and said, *I don't have time to contact a doctor and you need two pints of blood. Do you give me permission?*

"Do what you've got to do, I answered.

"I realized that this might be the very end. They often say that you don't panic when it's the end. I thought, my gory, I've got no kicks. I only feel sorry for my family. But I wasn't feeling sorry for myself. I knew God didn't need me, or my writing.

"I made it through the night. The next morning I was scheduled for exploratory surgery. Strangely, the bleeding had stopped. Within twenty-four hours I was feeling better. The day after that, I was released. When I was leaving the hospital, the nurse who had saved my life told me that I'd lost all resistance. If anybody had even breathed on me wrong, I might have died."

Dad seemed to be handling today's situation much like he had in the past: calm and self-assured.

Are your thoughts any different today?

"Not really. I've never been afraid of dying. It's never panicked me, but it's different now. Before I lost Rhoda, I never dwelled on it, but the fact is that I've had to come to terms with my own mortality," he said.

Perhaps this was a clue as to what was really going on with Dad. Confronting his own mortality had gotten the better of him. Yet his words didn't seem to reflect what was really happening.

"When you're younger," he continued, "the thought of dying is something a little scarier. When I had gastritis and thought is was the end, I had to rationalize why I might have to leave this world early. When you're my age, it's not a question of leaving early. I know that I've had fifty good years of marriage, watched my kids grow up, have grandchildren and all that. Anything I get from here on is an extra blessing."

I don't think I'd be quite as calm as you.

"You know, your brother Rick said the very same thing. Just like you, he didn't think he would be too calm either. So I'll tell you what I told him: It's all in your perspective. At my age, I can say I've already led a good life, full of blessings, and I'm willing to accept my own mortality. I know that I'm not going to be here forever. It's a more realistic view."

He paused for a moment, then added, "Heck, over a third of my high school classmates have already passed away. But don't get too worried; the preliminary indications are that what I've experienced will not be life threatening. So for right now, there's no cause for panic."

When did you begin handling your worries like this?

"When I was in the hospital after falling down the elevator shaft, I began asking myself, *How come I'm not worried? How come I'm not upset? Why don't things bother me?* Not that it was a bad thing. I was fortunate, because it's no fun to worry or to be anxious.

"Lying in that hospital bed, after much thought, I came to the conclusion that the reason I wasn't upset was because of my spiritual faith. After all, faith is an antidote for fear. I have courage because I've always been convinced that there is a spiritual power far greater than myself protecting me. The length of my life is beyond my control. The one thing within my control is doing my part. I knew I had things I had to do in this world. I had a mission. I had a purpose. My job was to complete that mission—however long or short. I filled the void of uncertainty with faith, and left no room for worry."

So you've delegated your worries to God. Isn't that blind faith?

"You could say I've delegated my worries, but not with total blindness. I still have to do my part. I can't cross the street without looking both ways.

"Faith is almost blind. And with this faith, I believe that things are going to work out for the best, even at the very edge of the precipice. Faith is optimism. It provides certainty in the face of uncertainty. It's what helps me maintain peace of mind, even under the most trying circumstances."

Just then, Marisa put her hands on the glass of the closed French door and peeked in.

Come in and talk to Grandpa, I shouted.

She entered and picked up the telephone.

"Hello, Grandpa Alligator," she said, using her pet name for Grandpa Al.

While they talked, I wondered what advice Dad would give to someone who didn't have spiritual faith. But I already knew. He'd probably recommend working on a project, getting absorbed in a hobby, or focusing on helping others. He'd say, *Keep busy because an idle mind is fertile soil for worry.*

Marisa handed the telephone back to me and disappeared as quickly as she had arrived.

Well hello, Grandpa Alligator, I mimicked affectionately.

"Do you know what day it is today?" he asked.

June 26th, I answered.

"Well, fifty-one years ago today I went on my first date with Rhoda. We went to see Guy Lombardo and his Royal Canadian Orchestra. We celebrated this day every year."

Well, if Rhoda wanted to touch your heart today, she had an interesting way of doing it, I said.

"She picked the right day, all right."

Or maybe you just wanted some time off from your writing.

"That seems to be the way to do it," he answered.

He filled me in on the tests that were scheduled, discussing them in a manner that sounded as if it were part of his normal routine. We talked for a while longer. Then it was time for Dad to get some rest. He wasn't worried—or so I thought.

As it turned out, Dad was just fine. All tests proved negative and, except for the ongoing need to manage his blood pressure, he was in pretty good health. However, what we all had come to realize was that Dad's formula for handling fear and worry was no longer working for him.

Sure, Dad was still able to delegate his largest worries to God. However, his strategy for handling life's daily challenges was no longer available. Mom was gone. He didn't even notice that these worries were accumulating. It was stress that brought him to the hospital that day.

This was something I told him during one of our routine phone calls about a year later: It's not that your hospital stay was self-inflicted, but you know that the stress of Mom's death, as well as her not being around to handle a host of items for you, became problematic. I believe your worries got out of proportion, which was totally out of character for you.

"Oh, yeah. That's true. You know, I gave it a lot of thought. I don't consider myself a worrier, never have. Yet I was very anxious and didn't realize it. I have no reason to exaggerate this because I want to give you an accurate picture, but I believe I was consumed with loneliness, and the old rules and old techniques weren't working."

I think you were off-balance. It's no secret that you had delegated most things to Mom, including the job of worrying.

"That's what she wanted, and I became very comfortable with it.

"But the big issue was depression. Bud thought I was in a state of depression," Dad said softly. "Of course, I denied it."

He paused to consider the idea.

"Now that I think back on it, he was right. I'm not talking about extreme depression; but there's no question about it, I was out-of-sync. I was worried about my own health and perhaps fixated on my own mortality. I became super-sensitive about symptoms.

"Here's the part I didn't recognize. It was the loneliness. I guess I didn't realize it went so deep. When I'd sit down to supper at night, there was no enjoyment of the food. I didn't even look forward to it, because Rhoda wasn't there. It was the companionship I missed. That's what created the phenomenal loneliness. That's what made me more negative and more sensitive about a host of smaller issues, including my own health. Now that I'm aware of these issues, I can once again handle any worry or anxiety that comes my way."

Walk 9 – Cooperate with the Healing Process

In late July 2001, Bud asked me to travel to Bangor to work out the details of Mom's estate. During the visit, my brothers, Dad, and I drove to Bar Harbor, a little over an hour east of Bangor. This was one of Mom's favorite places.

Mom had enjoyed our childhood treks to Bar Harbor and the coast. She particularly loved the drive through Acadia National Park, and her favorite stop along the way was Jordan Pond and the Jordan Pond House, where she'd order tea and popovers.

Jordan Pond is more like a lake than a pond, with crystal clear waters lapping over the pink speckled granite boulders forming its basin. Mom would often sit on a bench at the shore while we hiked the nearby carriage paths or skipped stones through the reedy shallows of the pond.

The Jordan Pond House dates back to the early 1900s. It opened as an overnight hotel, but later became a restaurant when it was purchased and incorporated into the Park. When you walk into the lodge with its big open-air dining room, fieldstone fireplace, and large windows looking over the pond and to the mountains beyond, it's easy to see why Mom kept coming back.

On this weekend the dining room was full. We left our name with the maitre d', happy to wait the half hour or so it would take until a table was available. Bud and Rick browsed the gift shop and waited to be called, while Dad and I headed towards the pond.

We walked the familiar path to the water. Wild blueberries dotted the field between the overgrown brush and boulders. After a couple of minutes we arrived at the pond. Dad watched me skip a couple of stones.

"What's on your mind today, Young Fella?"

Do you mind if we talk about how you've been doing since losing Mom? I began.

"Nah, not a bit. I seem to have a pretty good handle on things these days," he replied confidently.

So tell me what you've experienced, I said, as I looked for another smooth stone, avoiding eye contact.

"Well, initially I was in shock—no question about it. Or maybe it was denial, repression, or a combination of those things. Whatever you want to call it, that first period offered some protection. It allowed me to handle the initial trauma."

When did the shock wear off?

"It didn't take long for reality to set in. You see, the first ten days or so after Rhoda died, there was a lot of activity and distraction as I was surrounded with you guys and everybody else, which was helpful. When I returned home from Montreal, however, the shock or the numbness wore off pretty quickly, and I found myself alone. I wasn't prepared for the loneliness. Remember, I hadn't really been on my own for over fifty years," he said with a shrug.

"I found that even my *Twenty-Four Hour Rule* wasn't working for me."

What's your Twenty-Four Hour Rule?

"It's a rule that allows me to take time to let off some steam and go through the emotions of being upset, angry, or annoyed. It's something that usually happens overnight: I accept whatever has happened, appreciate the things I have, and then begin to find a *Constructive Compensation* to help me adjust to my new circumstances."

Dad described constructive compensation as one of the most powerful tools of adjustment. It's what helps him get up when he's knocked down. It's a technique, almost a mindset, for adjustment, which allows him to tolerate or conquer almost any negative that comes his way.

"Whether it's failure, disappointment, or pain, I insist on looking for a silver lining. It obligates me to compensate for my loss and find a substitute for the negative," Dad said.

"We all get our share of the negative. In fact, I believe it's what leads to personal growth. Constructive compensation is there to help us enjoy every drop of living possible. It allows us to gain from the wealth of our experience beyond the poverty of our loss. It asks us to find another blessing when one is lost and attempts to fill that vacuum. And, in the end, challenges are overcome and life can become even sweeter."

So what compensation did you find?

"I haven't been able to find a compensation for the loss of Rhoda, though one thing seemed to help. I was comforted with the spiritual connection I seem to have with your mom. There were a couple of incidents that occurred that let me know she was still with me, that she was watching over me. One night a light shone on my ceiling and a red bird appeared to fly across the room. Then there were several times in the evening when one of my lights went from dim to bright without me even touching it. I can't explain it, but it made me feel like Rhoda was present. At least that's how I chose to interpret it.

"You know what I'm talking about. You experienced something similar yourself," Dad reminded me.

That's right, I thought. I had told Dad about a couple of odd occurrences. Once, I was awakened by Mom's voice telling me, *Everything is going to work out well for you in life.* At the time, I remembered asking the voice, How do I know it's really you? Then I woke up at exactly 2:22 a.m.—one of Dad's lucky numbers.

Another time I awoke to what sounded like Mom's voice calling my name. This time I asked, Why have you come? And the voice answered, *I have come to visit with you.* These events were a little unsettling for me, yet they somehow seemed to help. I felt as if she were still with us.

"And as we've discussed," Dad continued, "we don't know whether they were real or imaginary, but at the time they provided some comfort. I like to think she's still watching over us."

We continued down the path toward Mom's favorite bench at the south end of the pond. Two large slabs of gray granite were pieced together here in 1915 to form the bench. A small memorial plaque now attached to the back reads: "In Grateful Loving Memory of Sarah Eliza Sigourney Cushing" who "dearly loved this spot."

Dad faced the bench with his hands in his pockets, reading the plaque.

"Rhoda really loved it here, too," he said quietly.

We sat for a while. Mixed along the steep hillsides are white paper birches, spruce, cedar, hemlock, and white pine. It's a forest still in recovery from a great fire that swept though here in the early 1940s, although there are no obvious scars. The North and South Bubbles, two rounded remnants of the glaciers, sit directly on the north end of the pond. The evidence of rockslides to our west is visible on the cliffs of Sargent and Penobscot Mountains. Another lake in miniature, Sargent Pond, is nestled in the upper elevations between those two mountains. Pemetic Mountain to the east completes the circle of granite ringing the pond and sheltering it from the harsh ocean winds not far away.

We renewed our discussion.

"What I found," Dad continued slowly, "was that the normal rules didn't apply anymore. There was no compensation for losing Rhoda. I was depressed. Almost every night for six months I went to bed saying, I don't care if I wake up tomorrow."

I didn't realize you were in such bad shape, I commented. Someone who's saying they don't care if they wake up the next morning—that's pretty serious.

"Agreed. Yet this happened to me many nights, if not every night," Dad reiterated.

If your morning routine included prayers of appreciation, how can you explain not caring if you didn't wake up again the next day?

"Because of the simple fact that I was being honest about my feelings. And the one thing I knew for sure was, no matter how bad it got at night, in the morning I'd be back in the fight. I found the sadness and depression were an evening thing for me, as I was able to stay so occupied during the day.

"So I allowed myself to be human and to express my own real feelings that I didn't care if I woke up the next day. But even after making such a statement, I would always remind myself at the very end that I've got a wonderful family and I've got my writing to complete. And that was generally the last word," Dad explained.

Were you at all prepared for this?

"One thing's for sure: I didn't realize how empty life was going to be. I wasn't prepared for the loneliness."

So what helped you? You seem to be in good shape now.

"My greatest therapy besides my morning sessions, by far, are the phone calls from you guys. When you talk about the healing process, I'm fortunate you are all around to help. Every day, when I get up, I know I'm going to get that call from Rick at six-thirty or quarter to seven; then Bud comes through mid-morning; and you finish it off with an evening call. You don't have any idea how much those calls mean to me. A lot of times in the evening when you called I'd have tears in my eyes because I was lonely. That wasn't therapy I went out to get— that was therapy that found me—and I appreciate it," he said, patting me on the shoulder.

I'm glad we were able to help you, I said, feeling pleased with having kept my promise made at Mom's funeral.

"As I think back," Dad continued, "one of the first things I did when I returned from Montreal was to give away most of Rhoda's belongings. I considered material possessions as reminders of the physical contact that I could no longer have with her. Items such as clothing, shoes, and the like were the kind of reminders I needed to have removed. Besides, I knew they could be used for a more constructive purpose. The thought of helping others made me feel good. So I gave all of those items away to charity. The only things I kept were pictures.

"I was also cautious about music. I couldn't turn on my favorite songs, especially Guy Lombardo. Music only brought back the loneliness.

"That's when I decided that I may not be happy, but I'm going to get up each day and get back into the challenge of writing. You see, when Rhoda had gotten sick last summer, I'd almost completely stopped writing. That was probably my first extended break from writing in almost fifty years.

"I began to shift my routine. I found value even from mundane challenges. I began paying my bills, doing the laundry, and showering in the evening. Eventually, I changed my whole schedule. These things occupied me and filled a little bit of the vacuum. When that didn't fully work, I would write till ten o'clock at night. One time I even wrote until two in the morning," he said, amazed with himself.

"On really tough days, I'd review my balance sheet and put the negative things on one side and the positives on the other. Then I would remind myself that I live in one of the greatest countries in the world, with a roof over my head, enough to eat, access to healthcare, modern conveniences, and the ability to earn a decent living. I'm free to express my opinions, travel, and to practice the religion of my choice. That's better than three-quarters of the people in the world. I've also had seventy-four great years, including fifty years with a wonderful wife. I enjoy my writing every day and above all—I consider this my greatest blessing—my three sons. When I looked at my balance sheet, I'm so far ahead that if I had left this world twenty-five years ago, I'd have had no kicks."

There was another thing that I knew helped Dad. A few months back, Dad had decided to sponsor a child through Save the Children. Her name was Harleen and helping this child lifted Dad's spirit.

Does Harleen help?

"Absolutely, I feel very good about that gal. It's been healing. When you've lost somebody, you've got to continue to have things that make you feel as if you've still got a purpose in life. This is my chance to help someone who really needs it. And it makes me feel as if I'm doing something worthwhile."

Then Dad said excitedly, "You know, I got a letter from her."

Really. What did it say?

"I'll have to read it to you sometime. I really appreciated hearing from her."

Was this any kind of compensation for losing Mom?

"No. But I've compensated for the loneliness in several ways and love has returned. And that was the turning point. That was the insight that made all the difference. I realized I had to go through grieving. I had to go through depression. Death is not convenient, nor predictable. I understood that some of the old rules, that had helped me adjust, no longer applied. I began to ask myself, why do things have to be the way they used to be? Why not build a life around what really exists? Why should I seek the same contentment that I had before? That's when I really started counting my blessings. I was fortunate for the seventy-four great years I had been given and thought maybe the next few years wouldn't be as great, but they could still be loaded with purpose. I still had my family, and I still had my writing.

"So, I decided to work with what I had. I began to cooperate with the healing process. I realized that no matter how tough things got, I had to appreciate the things I had, to accept the hand that was dealt, and to improve upon it by adjusting to the new situation.

"Since then—except for the absence of Rhoda—my life is almost as challenging and exciting as it used to be. I don't believe I'm a sad person anymore.

"Now I consider Rhoda my spiritual partner. You see, we don't know what happens to a person when they die. We can have a negative view and say they're put in the ground and that's the end, or we can have a positive view and allow them to remain with us. My compensation for Rhoda's loss allows me to believe that she is still with me.

"I believe that Rhoda goes to all the Red Sox ball games. Better than that, she gets in for free," he said with a smile. "I also believe she doesn't miss any skating matches and probably goes to every Dollar Store she can find. And, of course, she's watching over us guys very carefully."

Our conversation ended and we headed back towards the main lodge to see if our table was ready. As we walked back up the little path, Dad said, "You know, Bud gets a kick out of the things I refer to as *tidbits from the trashcan of knowledge.* Here's a tidbit for you. It's a little tradition that Rhoda and

I always enjoyed, one that I don't think anybody else in the family knew."

What's that?

"You know the collection of little ceramic elephants that we have in the living room. We loved those elephants," he said nostalgically. "Sometimes, Rhoda would say good night to them. Now, on occasion, I go over and look at those elephants and say, I'm not going to forget you, Rhoda, from the smallest elephant to the largest, from the littlest thing to the biggest. You'll always be with me."

A few days later, while speaking on the phone with Dad, I reminded him about Harleen's letter.

"Do you want me to read it to you?" Dad asked.

Sure, I answered.

"Hold on, I'll get it," he said, setting down the receiver. I could hear him scurrying around, opening and shutting drawers as he tried to find the letter.

He got back on the line and asked, "Are you still there?"

I'm right here.

"Okay," he began, "the fact is, it's written in part English and part Philipino, but down below it's translated. She writes:

Dear Grandpa Al:

Hello. Have a nice day. Wishing you good health.

Thank you for sending me a birthday card. I was very surprised. I hope you will not grow tired of writing to me.

I've seen your photo together with your family. It is very nice to see, especially your grandsons and granddaughter in the picture. I will always pray for you to our Lord. I hope to see you soon. Bye bye for now. You are the most wonderful Grandpa Al I ever had.

Love,

Harleen

"How's that for a gal who's only seven years old?"

She sounds pretty special.

"She's special all right. Oh, by the way, I also received a letter from the caseworker who sort of apologized for Harleen's religious-sounding message. She must have been referring to the part where Harleen wrote, *I'm praying for you*." he said.

You obviously didn't mind, did you?

"Nah. In fact, I wrote a letter back to her, probably about a month ago, in which I said, I think it's wonderful that you're praying, because praying helps to make a better world."

Just think, I said, with a hint of amazement, this child from halfway around the world is praying for you.

"It's humbling. But you know, I need it," he said softly. "Actually, we all need to pray and to have others pray for us. It helps us appreciate our blessings.

"In fact, I've come to recognize that even pleasant memories are blessings. I never would have believed it possible. When Rhoda first died, people would tell me, *Someday you'll have pleasant memories of her*. I'd wonder, are they kidding? I knew they were only trying to be nice, but what pleasant memories were they talking about? Pleasant memories of losing her? I didn't see how there could ever be pleasant memories again.

"Then after several months, I realized, wait a minute, I'm not really leaving Rhoda behind. She's still with me. Just about every day now, I go to one of her pictures and remind myself of a pleasant memory.

"When I look at our wedding picture above our bed," Dad continued, "I think about when we first got married and were living in Boston. She didn't like Boston much as she was pretty young and missed her family back in Montreal. Still I remember that one of our big pleasures at the time was going out to dinner. Rhoda was working full time while I attended school. And every Monday it was 99¢ chicken down at a little restaurant on Tremont Street. Wednesday was Prince Spaghetti Day at the Prince Spaghetti House. Friday evening was the Causeway Cafeteria, a kosher-style restaurant where we had a type of stew called tzimmes. Nobody made a better tzimmes—not even Rhoda. And Saturday we had 10¢ hot dogs, with everything on it, at the hot dog stand.

"Now when I look at her picture, I frequently say, *You gave me fifty great years*. They were right; the pleasant memories do return."

Walk 10 – Spirituality: The Common Thread

Ten months had passed since Mom's death, and in August of 2001 we again traveled to Montreal, this time to unveil her gravestone. This ceremony is a tradition for Jews and is held within one year of a person's death. It signals the end of the formal mourning period.

We stayed at the Chateau Champlain. It's a big hotel with half-moon windows peering out to the city. Our room faced north, towards downtown. Church spires and old landmarks, like The Queen Elizabeth Hotel, share the skyline with modern office buildings. We could look beyond to Mount Royal, the highest point in the city. St. Joseph's Oratory sits on the mountain's flank, with its long staircase and enormous domed roof. Millions of people come here each year, some to seek their cure. In the lower reaches of the church are thousands of pairs of crutches, braces and wheelchairs left behind by the faithful.

When we were kids we stayed with friends or relatives on our summer trips to the city. We spent much of our time running among the houses of our extended family.

We'd go to the zoo or take a roller coaster ride at La Fontaine Park. Of course, we always made time for a stop at the Yang Zhe Restaurant on Van Horne for their egg rolls and spare ribs in a sticky garlic sauce. Sometimes we'd walk through the botanical gardens or down the cobblestone streets of Old Montreal along the St. Lawrence. In the distance we would see the big glass dome of the US Pavilion from Expo '67.

If the Expos were in town, we'd go to Jarry Park and watch Rusty Staub play. Jarry Park was like no other and the customs of those in attendance were really quite foreign for baseball. Men and woman would be dressed in evening formal wear, drinking cocktails and dining on hors d'oeuvres. In right field, eight feet beyond the short fence, was a swimming pool. And many a home run would end up taking a dip along with a few kids who'd dive in for a souvenir. This was a far cry from our more familiar Fenway Park in Boston.

On this day Dad and I had planned on taking a morning walk. I waited for him in the lobby, seated in a comfortable oversized chair. I thought about his formula for happiness. What kept coming back to me was that spirituality was a central theme to every part of his life.

Dad arrived and greeted me. "Well hello, Young Fella."

He sat down in the chair next to me, and after a few minutes we set out for our walk. The bellman opened the door out onto the plaza and we crossed the covered drive at the front of the hotel on Rue Peel. There was the familiar buzz from Dad's hearing aids. He tested them by cupping his hands to each of his ears.

Montreal is such a great city, I said, as we crossed the street.

"I know what you mean," Dad said. "I get excited every time I cross the Champlain Bridge. I can't help but admire the beauty of this island city. Rhoda used to tell me the minute she crossed that bridge she felt like she was home."

We walked in silence for a couple of blocks and then I said, I was hoping you could clarify something for me.

"Okay," Dad replied. "What's the issue?"

You've always spoken so confidently about God, and your writings frequently refer to *the Cosmic Pattern, the Divine Design* or *the Perfect Plan*. How can you be so sure it exists?

"I have simply chosen to believe it exists," Dad answered. "When I consider the intricacy of how things work or the beauty of this world, to me, it couldn't be just an accident. But I have another belief you may find more rational: I believe in God because I'm practical. As I've told you before, nothing could be more beneficial. In fact, I consider having belief in a spiritual power healthy for the human condition."

Then what would you say to an atheist?

"I think atheism, life without faith in God, is limiting. Atheists deny themselves the tremendous payoff that comes only from having faith. Atheists can't reach out to a spiritual power for assistance. They're limited to their own human potential.

"It's tempting to wait for more evidence in order to believe in God, but finding scientific proof of God's existence may well be impossible. Though I can't prove anything to atheists, I would stress the value gained just through belief itself. But I wouldn't expect to change their minds. On the other hand, an atheist would have just as tough a time proving to me that God doesn't exist or that there is no value to believing in God. And though I receive a tremendous benefit just through belief, I still don't know that God exists, and I wouldn't dictate to anyone that they need to choose my beliefs," Dad emphasized.

You know, I've been working on your formula for happiness for some time now and I've drawn some conclusions. It appears that spiritual faith is the common thread of your writing and in what you routinely discuss. I'm sure you're well aware of this, but I thought you might appreciate my interpretation.

I could tell that he was very interested, like a proud teacher realizing the potential of his students at the end of the school year. We stopped at a traffic light at Boulevard René-Levesque and waited for it to change. We crossed the street and looked back at the Cathedral, a smaller replica of St. Peter's Basilica in Rome.

Wow, I said, look at that, as I pointed towards the row of saints lining the gabled rooftops on the outer building of the Marie Reine du Monde Cathedral.

Behind them rose the green dome and we paused to look at it for a moment and then continued on to Dorchester Square. We entered the park with its tall trees and benches, directly in the shadow of the Cathedral.

"You were saying," Dad said as he sat down.

Now remember, I began, this may be a bit simplistic, but it should capture your basic message. Let me know what you think.

"Okay. I'm ready when you are."

Here's how I would piece it together: You rise each morning with meditation, spiritual affirmations, smiling contemplation, and prayers. This is what helps you program your attitude for the day. It's something that creates a general sense of optimism within you, allowing you to maintain a positive attitude. It's the same method that prevents fear or worry from destroying your peace of mind.

Faith is something that assists you in making decisions. It's what helps you overcome the anxiety of indecision. In the process, you follow a moral code that insists on the fair treatment of others and asks you to always do your full part.

When things go your way, great! You can appreciate all the blessings you have in life. When things don't go your way, you still count your blessings and are thankful for what you've been given, in spite of your troubles. It's this combination of faith and appreciation that helps you to prepare for life's most difficult moments. It's what helps you accept your losses, even when they're beyond understanding. And it's this faith that in time gives you the ability to adjust to anything.

By walking the fine line between the spiritual and material worlds you are able to keep it all in balance. You are careful not to get caught in the endless cycle of craving material possessions. That's what allows you to give to others, and this provides you with a deeper meaning and purpose in life.

That's what I've learned. What do you think?

"You know," he added, "this is a great gift. The way you've presented my concepts makes me feel that you're my teacher now. And I thank you. That's my comment, Young Fella."

Isn't there anything you would change?

"Well, there is one more point I want to stress and that's the distinction between believing and knowing."

Isn't that just semantics?

"It's more than that to me. Beliefs are peaceful, but people who claim to *know* are the basis for most religious conflict and have been the cause of much bloodshed over the years.

"What I've found is that by being able to admit that these are simply my *beliefs*, I remain open to the beliefs of others. However, suppose I were to say that I *know* there is only one right way, or one right religion. Then I would be challenging all those who have different beliefs.

"It's arrogant to claim to know all the answers to life's unanswerable questions. For me, I feel a lot more comfortable offering my beliefs on the subject, and I'm very cautious when claiming to know."

We headed back to our hotel to get ready for the ceremony.

"There's still one more thing, and that's consistency," Dad offered. "Going to church on Sunday or to synagogue on Saturday is nice, but it's not necessarily spirituality. Spirituality is available seven days a week and can be found anywhere at any time."

Well, if consistency is important, is there a particular religion that you recommend? I asked.

"The best place to start is with your own religion. Start with your roots and the religious traditions you grew up with. Or use your own personal beliefs. Either way, this should help you to find peace of mind and is more likely to inspire a deeper faith.

"Of course, no one religion has cornered the market on faith or belief in God. Spiritual wealth is not limited to any one denomination or religion. Spirituality can be an entirely personal experience. And remember, this is what I *believe*. Nobody really knows for sure."

Later that morning we headed to the cemetery. We were the first to arrive and wandered around for a little while in our family's section. Mom is buried near her parents, Esther and Sam Sondon. Five of Esther's six siblings are also buried there, along with their parents.

My grandmother Esther was killed by a hit-and-run driver in 1964. Mom would later replace her as the cornerstone for the family. As it turned out, Mom was the first of her generation to die. Most of her cousins were in attendance. As they arrived, they would go to the graves of their parents and other relatives, stopping to put some blades of grass or small stones on top of the headstones as a symbol of their remembrance.

As family and friends were assembling, Dad and I approached Mom's grave. Red impatiens lined the path. The headstone was covered with a white cloth, which would soon be removed. I stood directly in front of Mom's stone, with Kari and Marisa on one side and Dad on the other. Rick and his family, Bud, and Uncle Warren and his family were among us.

Since it's customary for someone to say a few words, Dad planned to speak. I thought back to the funeral with some guilt, remembering that Dad had wanted to speak at the time.

While Dad was reviewing the few words he would say on this day, I asked him if he remembered how we'd coaxed him out of speaking at the funeral.

"Oh, yeah," he answered.

Did that bother you?

"No," he said, without hesitation.

How come?

"Because I respected your opinions. I wanted to make it a moment that everyone would be comfortable with, and, if that's how you guys felt, it was okay with me. It wasn't a necessity for me to speak," he said calmly.

Really?

"Well, I would have preferred it," he responded, "but it was okay. Besides, I can speak today."

I still feel a little guilty about it, I said.

"You don't have to feel guilty about it, Young Fella. That was the consensus, so it was fine with me. I'm still trying to get rid of the guilt I have for spanking you that time you threw your boot at the nursery school teacher."

He grinned at me, and somehow I felt better.

The Rabbi removed the white cloth revealing Mom's headstone. It was simple, with Mom's name in English and Hebrew, the dates of her birth and death, and a small Star of David carved into the gray granite. Across the bottom was written:

"Forever Loved   Forever Remembered   Forever Cherished"

The stone was cut wide to accommodate two names. I read Mom's name in the bright sunlight and saw Dad's shadow darkening the other half of the stone that would eventually bear his name.

We stood there quietly as the Rabbi read some prayers. I was wondering what was going through Dad's mind.

Later, he told me what he had been thinking.

"Here is Rhoda's final resting place, and I have a choice to make: I have to decide whether to believe she's gone into the ground forever and I'll never see her again, or to believe she's living on in the spiritual world. And I reaffirmed right there to believe she lives on," he said.

The Rabbi spoke, and we recited the mourners' prayer. Then Dad stepped forward.

"First, I want to thank everyone who has come here this morning to honor Rhoda," he said, looking fondly at the people who'd gathered.

"I was told that it's customary to say a few words at an unveiling, so, I'll talk to Rhoda today," he said, turning towards Mom's headstone.

"Rhoda, you were a phenomenal cook."

I knew Dad was being serious, but he got a few laughs, and I wondered somewhat uncomfortably what he was going to say next.

He continued, "But that is not what I miss."

He paused.

"It's not even the affection. What I miss is the companionship of sitting down and talking with you about our problems. I miss looking after you and making sure that no one upset you or hurt your feelings. I miss the time spent together at the end of the day sharing a cup of tea."

Again he paused.

"I thank you for being my good companion. I thank you for keeping our family close. I thank you for fifty good years of marriage."

Then he closed his eyes and said, "Until we meet again, Rhoda—until we meet again, you will always be my close spiritual companion."

Walk 11 – The Artistic Fine Line

Our return trip from Montreal again brought us through the western mountains of Maine. This was where we went our separate ways. Just after Grafton Notch, Rick, Heather and their kids headed east to Bangor and the rest of us turned south, towards Portland, to spend a few days at Bud's in Naples.

We had a good night's rest at Bud's home. The next day we set out to visit our friends, Gio and Jim, who were vacationing on Peaks Island, one of the more than three hundred so-called "Calendar Islands" in Casco Bay. We took the 20-minute ferry ride from Portland. It was an uncommonly hot, sunny day for Maine, well over 90 degrees. Even just a hundred yards from shore, the breeze off the cool ocean made things a lot more comfortable.

A playful seal greeted us as we approached the island. Our friends were there as well, waiting for us at the pier. We said our hellos at the dock. Then we walked past a park in the little town center and piled into their station wagon for the two-minute drive to their cottage.

The island's commercial district is directly up a hill. There is a small general store that sells ice cream and souvenirs, a bicycle rental shop, and a couple of restaurants. We made a brief stop at Gio and Jim's to drop off our things, and then we began to explore the island.

Peaks Island is an interesting mix of tall trees, Victorian cottages and all manner of other summer homes. The front half of the island is older and looks like an artists' colony. The back half is rougher, with a rocky coastline facing the open sea and the islands beyond. In recent years there has been some development on this side of the island to take advantage of the views, but it's very difficult and expensive to accomplish. One home has been uniquely built on top of an abandoned cement battery that was placed there during World War II to defend the bay.

My impression of island living is that everything is unusual. It looks different. It feels different. There's a certain look to the people. They're more fit, with women wearing flowing dresses and men with groomed beards. The mood is softer. It's a place where people escape, like we were doing.

We stopped the car and parked it in a small spot hidden among some thick Rugosa rose bushes. Dad and I climbed down the weathered gray granite towards the water. We sat down and talked, all the while keeping an eye on Marisa, who was up ahead of us, already playing in a pool of water left behind by the retreating tide.

I'm glad we're getting a chance to talk today, I said.

"Why's that?"

I want to discuss one of your strengths, and that's dealing with people.

"Okay," he said, "what do you want to know?"

You have this great way with people. How do you do it?

"What I've discovered over time is that there is a fine line between success and failure. It's something I refer to as *The Artistic Fine Line*. Sometimes the line is so slight it's almost imperceptible. In dealing with people, like anything else, the artistic fine line is often right in front of you, yet still illusive. For me, it's that little bit of extra patience and humor that makes all the difference. Sometimes it's a simple process, other times it's more of a challenge.

"Let me give you an example. One day, while working at Viner Music Company, this guy came in yelling, *There's the crook who sold me my color television set.*

"Now remember, this was done in front of a lot of customers, so it came as a bit of a shock to me. But I can generally handle things when I'm attacked, and I didn't let it bother me. Instead, I went up to him and said, *Look, I'm not going to dispute one thing that you're saying. Why don't we go into my office, sit down, and talk this over?*

"He was glad to do it, and I wanted him off the floor where he was disturbing other customers. Once we were in my office, I asked him, *What's the problem?* He explained that he bought a television set from us six months earlier and the picture tube went dead. I said, *No problem, it's under warranty. You've got a year of free service and two years on the tube. We don't charge for delivery, so you're all set.*

"He said, *No, that's not what I want. I want a brand new television set.* I asked him, *Why do you want a new one?* He answered, *Well, the fact is, your company brought that television set down my bumpy road in East Eddington, and I think that's how it got damaged.*

"I asked him, *What do you want us to do with the old one?* And he said, *Oh, listen. I've kept it in great condition, so you won't have any problem selling it to someone else.*

"Then I asked him, *Would you really want to deal with a company that sold used TVs as if they were new?* And he merely said, *Well, that's your problem.*

"Finally, he said, *If you don't give me a brand new television set, you're going to hear from my lawyer.*"

Why would he want to get his lawyer involved? I asked.

"I didn't think he had a leg to stand on, but I realized I wasn't getting through to him. So I took a slightly different approach. That's where the artistic fine line comes in. For me, it's humor.

"Then I said, *Okay, I agree with you, I think you should have a brand new television set. And by the way, you'll be hearing from our lawyer.* The guy was dumbfounded and asked why.

"And I said, *Any guy that has the nerve to ask us to drive down that rocky road to East Eddington knows that we might damage our delivery truck's engine. But I'm not going to have our lawyer sue you for just the engine. No, I'm going to have him sue you for a brand new truck.* Then I smiled.

"Well, this guy laughed, shook his head and said, *Okay. Get that set fixed.* From then on, whenever he'd come into the store the first guy he'd talk to was me."

That's why I don't mess around with you, I said.

"Of course you know, humor is a dangerous tool. It's got to be used cautiously, because there's a fine line that separates humor from insult. You never know how it's going to be taken. In this case, I didn't have much to lose. The thing is, it worked.

And it demonstrated the fine line between an angry customer and a happy customer.

"You know, Rick said that he thinks I generally follow Dale Carnegie's method of dealing with people, and he wondered if there's anything I do that's original. Of course, we learn from others. But the artistic fine line is something I've developed. If I encounter a particularly difficult situation, I try to determine the subtle change that will make all the difference. At other times, the artistic fine line may be willpower or that extra bit of energy that helps me overcome obstacles.

"At the same time, artists are aware of their limitations and imperfections. An artist recognizes that progress is made through concentrating on strengths and compensating for weaknesses. And when all else fails, it's understanding that as humans we can utilize our faith as a supplement," Dad stated.

This sounds a lot like self-discipline, I offered, gazing at Marisa happily playing in her saltwater pool.

"That's right. And the difference between success and failure is bridged by self-discipline. Look at Michael Jordan or Larry Bird. If they had a poor basketball game, it could be midnight, but they're going to be in the gym shooting baskets for hours. Even when they're tired, they're practicing. That's the fine line difference between the good and the great. Of course, I don't shoot baskets. I just have this corny sense of humor."

Michael Jordan is amazing, I said. He really demonstrates the desire for excellence. I understand he built a professional basketball court in his home. Did you know he has his own personal trainer and chef? Now, that's an artist.

"You know, basketball is a great example," Dad continued. "Like most sports, the game often is decided by one point. For that matter, the outcome of an entire season can come down to the final few seconds. You can see it's a fine line that separates victory from defeat," he reiterated.

"But you don't have to strive for perfection, nor do you need to be as successful as Michael Jordan. The key is to constantly seek to improve," he said.

"Another thing for you to consider is focus. Focus gives us the ability to concentrate on the critical details. From what I've witnessed, artists have incredible focus and attention to detail. They take nothing for granted and constantly hone their skills. They realize that the simplest error can alter the most delicate of brush strokes or one omission can change the whole picture," Dad warned.

Do you have an example of this?

"Sure. Have I ever told you about Thomas Edison?"

I don't think so, I said.

"Okay, here's the story," Dad said, as if Edison were a personal friend.

"You may not know this, but there were several other scientists working on creating the light bulb. It was recognized that electricity gave light, so it was a reasonable assumption that if properly harnessed, it could provide light on demand. The other scientists working on this concept were every bit as brilliant as Thomas Edison, but how did he beat them to the punch?" Dad asked.

"How did he beat them?" he repeated.

"The fact is, one of those other scientists actually had a better light bulb, with a better filament. But the difference between Thomas Edison and these others was that all the other scientists were pure scientists; whereas, Tom Edison was not only a scientist, he was an entrepreneur. He had made arrangements for financial backing and established a strong business network. This allowed him to hire the best scientist he could find as an assistant. Once he discovered a light bulb that worked, he enlisted his business network to build a factory to manufacture the product. He also had the money to promote it as well. While another scientist may have created the first light bulb, he had no ability to bring it to market, and history has rewarded Edison and given him credit for the invention.

"Patience and persistence are also very important. The artist has the mindset of a marathoner and recognizes that every race is run one step at a time. When tired or thinking about letting up, the artist has patience to endure. During the last mile, which is usually the toughest, the artist has that little bit extra for the finish line.

"All I ever want to do is the best job possible. I try not to leave things to chance. That way I have no regrets."

Does this apply in the business world as well? I asked.

"Look," Dad answered, "it can be applied in any field. Whether it's used in business, basketball, or in the spiritual realm, the artistic fine line still applies. Though, as you know, I happen to use it for spiritual growth, not for accumulating material wealth."

I understand that all too well, I responded. But I can see how this principle is applicable towards succeeding at anything.

Dad nodded his head in agreement, then said, "By following a spiritual path in life you can apply the formula in any situation. I look at my life as if I'm a musician in a vast orchestra. My job is to sharpen my skills, playing each note artfully. The beauty of the symphony is the artistic combination of the various instruments. Remember," Dad cautioned, "it's an art, not a science."

I stood up and wandered towards Marisa. Dad followed closely behind. Our sudden movement startled a seagull that had been perched on the rocks in front of us. It flew out over the water in the direction of a passing schooner. I was about to point out the boat to Marisa when I noticed she was already waving to its crew.

Dad said, "I've got something else to discuss with you."

What's on your mind today, Young Fella? I responded.

"What do you think about me taking an apartment at Boyd Place?"

He explained that Boyd Place was the independent living section of the Phillips-Strickland House in Bangor, which had a very good reputation. He insisted that nothing would really change, except for his meals. Breakfast and dinner were served in a common dining room. This would offer him some companionship.

What made you consider this? I asked.

"Well, as you know, I'm not much of a cook and there's only so many ways you can prepare tuna or lima beans," he said with a laugh. "But seriously, Rick thought it might be a good idea for me to take a look. So I toured it a couple of weeks ago."

What did you think?

"It seemed pretty nice," he answered.

How does it work?

"I get my own apartment and I can keep my car. Meals are prepared for me in the dining room and there are some common areas, like a library and exercise room. Then someday, should I need more assistance, or need full time care at their nursing home, I'm already a resident. It's not like I'd be giving up my independence. Besides, it's probably best for me to look into something like this before I really need it. What do you think?"

I thought for a moment and then answered, if I were in your shoes, I'd check it out thoroughly. Certainly, there's nothing wrong with exploring it. But be careful and make sure you talk to some people who live there to help you understand if it's right for you.

By this time, we had reached Marisa. Evidently, she had been listening to our conversation. Before Dad could respond, Marisa chimed in, "If I were in either of your shoes," and she paused for a moment to consider the advice she would give, "I would need smaller shoes," she said with a smile.

Listening to Marisa reminded me that I don't have all the answers; nobody does. Each of us has our own strengths and weaknesses and our own path in life.

Walk 12 - Finding Purpose

Dad took the apartment at Boyd Place, a move that would bring about some big changes. That became apparent in an evening phone conversation we had not long after he had settled there.

"Well hello, Young Fella. What's on your mind tonight?"

I'm checking up on you to see how you like your new apartment.

"It's better than I imagined. I have a really good feeling about this place. You know, I looked it over very carefully during a couple of visits last month. I met with the staff and learned I already knew some of the management here. They're good people. The atmosphere is friendly. And you should see the dining room," he said with excitement.

You seem pleased.

"Oh, yeah. It was the right thing to do. By the way, Bud was here today and helped me hang all my pictures. He has a good eye for those things. Next week I'm ordering new drapes. How about that?"

Have you ever picked out drapes before? I thought you were color-blind?

"I'm getting some help from a professional. Don't worry."

That apartment seems like the right place for you, I said.

"I think I was supposed to come here. Oh, and I'll tell you something else that has happened. Now that I'm closer to downtown, I've been going to the library most days just after lunch and bumped into Sara Thompson, an old friend of mine."

Really? An old friend, huh?

"No. No. No. It's not like that," he retorted, not the least bit amused. "I learned that she's been having a serious problem with diabetes. It was so severe that the pain nearly incapacitated her and she's had to give up her job. She was pretty depressed.

"She tells me that our daily discussions are helping her. Most days I meet her around two o'clock and spend half an hour or so talking with her. I look forward to it. I enjoy talking with her, making her laugh, telling her stories. I think it's helping bring her out of her depression. Most importantly, I discovered that by helping her, I've been helping myself.

"Sara and I have spoken about this, and we agree that my move to Boyd Place was meant to be. The timing was right so we could help each other."

Has helping Sara allowed you to find more meaning in your life?

"Sure. I know you've asked me about having a purpose in life. And when I consider the subject of purpose, I wonder, what's the purpose that keeps anybody going?"

He cleared his throat and continued.

"My answer has a little bit of a twist. It's actually a question. I ask, why not purpose? Since we don't live in the

Garden of Eden and this is not a perfect world, there are challenges to overcome. It's my belief that we are placed on this earth to help others. Giving to others provides satisfaction and meaning to our lives."

Is that what you recommend for everyone?

"I recommend doing what's comfortable for you," Dad answered. "Spiritually, this feels right to me. There's a Buddhist teaching on this subject, that a candle can light many other candles without shortening its own life. Happiness is only enhanced from being shared."

I've always been convinced that Dad's purpose in life is to help people with the philosophy he's developed over the years. A few months later I received a letter from Sara that reinforced my belief:

Dear Harley,

I'm sitting here at my kitchen table writing to you, listening to Billie Holiday. I can smell my flower garden outside the window and I'm thinking how happy I am. I'm not anxious and I'm not just killing time. This must be "living in the moment."

You know, your father has really lifted my spirits and I'm grateful for his friendship. He spends time with me almost every day, reads my mood, and says exactly what I need to hear. I'm sure he's told you about my diabetes. I wanted you to know how he's helped me come to terms with my illness and to find the spiritual person that I once was.

I feel compelled to write you, knowing how much you and your brothers love him. In particular, I know that you're working with him on his book and trying to capture his philosophy. Maybe I can give you some insight into how he impacts me.

First, let me back up and tell you about my recent history. My diabetes has been steadily advancing over the years. I've been receiving dialysis for some time now and it has been exhausting. A couple of months ago I had to give up my job and most everything else.

Along the way, I was fortunate to have met a very spiritual woman who had been dealing with this same illness for years. She took me under her wing, just as I was having thoughts of suicide. She talked about a deeper meaning to life, thoughts that were familiar to my own.

With her help, I began to find myself again. I started making notes on my experience and my feelings. I thought perhaps this journal could someday help others. At times, the words appeared to be gifts from God or from spiritual guides. I wasn't sure. All I knew was that it was helping me.

Just as this philosophy began to really take root in my mind and spirit, I ended up in the hospital with pneumonia. I remember lying in that hospital bed with an IV in my arm, wondering if I would ever be whole again. Somehow I recovered, but I was very depressed.

I had never experienced depression before— I had always been ecstatic about life. I was certain my former self was gone, yet somewhere deep inside I never gave up hope that I could once again enjoy life.

Bumping into your father at the library was really a Godsend. From the moment we sat down, I knew it was not just a mere coincidence that we ran into each other after all these years.

It only took a few conversations for us to understand that we spoke the same spiritual language and that we needed each other. I needed a friend and a teacher to help me understand my illness and why it happened to me. He needed an escape from loneliness—from missing your mom. Within a month, each of us had left depression behind.

Your father has helped me realize many things about life and about myself. He has given me the courage to find hope, and helped me overcome my fears. His philosophy has helped me to regain my spirituality and has taught me how to keep it all in balance.

I know that he's given you and your brothers these lessons your whole life. He lives his life according to these principles and from what he tells me, each of you follows a similar path. It's not surprising to hear that all three of you are just like him.

His philosophy is centered on love, which I know is his greatest gift. He listens to me and offers unconditional love. Forgive me if this seems too personal, I just wanted to let you know how special he is to me.

He has a certain vitality about him that washes over everyone he meets. It's something I can't adequately describe. He's not old—never will be. He's never lost his purpose in life, which from what I can tell seems to be what ages people. He told me the other day that this is the most exciting time for him in his life—the present.

Living in the present now seems to me like the only way to live, thanks to your dad.

Very Fondly,

Sara

I read Sara's letter to my dad the day I received it.

When I had finished reading it to him, I asked, Is there something special about Sara?

"We're just friends, if you're trying to get at something."

Would you say that living in the present has helped you stay focused on your purpose in life? I asked.

Dad paused for a moment to collect his thoughts.

"Maybe it's understanding that life is a journey," he answered mysteriously.

"Life is lived on the path—not just at the milestones. Think about it: ninety-nine percent of the time is spent on the road. The fleeting moments of success in life, or failure, for that matter, only occur at the end of the journey. So enjoy every step along the way. Success is not reaching the top of the mountain. It's being able to appreciate the climb. It's being able to measure the distance I've traveled from where I started. It's the progress, the setbacks, and the challenge. Whether it's defined as success or failure, it's my expression and spiritual belief that allows me to find purpose in everything I do," he said.

"As for purpose, I realize that the Good Lord doesn't need me, or my book. I'm not even sure if I'm going to finish it before I leave this world. Even if I do, there's no guarantee it will be successful. For me, the most satisfying self-expression—other than my three sons—is my writing. Just being able to write makes me happy, and the thought that my material could one day help others keeps life thrilling."

Then would you say writing is your mission?

"As long as I can remember, I've had a mission. I think it started when I was around the age of ten. I didn't know what it was. I just assumed that one day I would fulfill my mission, and then I'd know.

"I believed my mission was spiritual, not material. And that's why, even as a kid, I never felt the need to own things. Even to own a car. When I did get one, it was great, but I didn't see the need. I could live without a vehicle, even now. I could live without owning a home, too, and still have peace of mind. But my mission became clearer to me sometime during college. That's when I became determined to deliver a philosophy for living," Dad said.

Has it ever frustrated you that it's still a work in progress?

"I'm glad you asked that question, and I'll tell you why. I haven't been a bit frustrated. What has always kept me going was something I read by Milton: *He serves who only stands and waits*."

But you've been waiting over fifty years, I insisted.

"I have to admit this—call it my spiritual fantasy if you wish—but I've always believed that because I enjoy writing so much and was never in a rush to get it done, the spiritual forces would bring along the events that would get these words out at the right time."

After a slight pause he said, "You may happen to be *the event*, Young Fella."

We're making good progress, I confirmed.

"You're making such progress with the book, I can picture it finished and talking to people about it. Now I'm wondering, am I prepared?"

Well, are you?

"I hope so," he said with a hearty laugh.

Hasn't fifty years of preparation been enough?

"We'll just have to wait and see."

Walk 13 – Attunement

Dad came to Virginia for Thanksgiving 2001. It had been only a few months since my last walk with Dad, yet our world had been transformed in the interim by the September 11th attacks.

Our friends the Behnkes joined us at our house for dinner. The turkey was ready and the dining room table was prepared. This was the same table that had been in my parents' house when I was a kid.

Mom had always wanted a dining room, and after twelve years on Lancaster Avenue, she finally got her wish. A dining room was added to our small home. Not long after the room was completed, a French provincial dining set arrived: a table with inlaid wood, matching chairs, and china cabinet. Uncle Warren added a final touch and gave her a chandelier. She was thrilled. Mom wasn't a materialistic person, but this room really meant something to her. And when my parents sold their home and moved into an apartment, I received that dining room set.

Before serving our meal we offered a prayer. We prayed for the many families who had suffered the loss of a loved one. We prayed for America and asked for the courage to face those who threaten us, justice for those who were guilty, and, even more importantly, justice for those who were wrongfully accused. And we prayed for the innocent victims of despair living throughout the world.

The next morning Dad and I got up early and went for a walk. It was a quiet morning except for the fluttering sounds of birds at the feeder in our front yard. The air was cool, with the sweet aroma of smoke from a neighbor's fireplace.

After a few minutes we reached the Washington & Old Dominion Trail. It was once a railroad track, but is now paved and serves as a walking path. Still, it was easy to picture trains steaming through. A gravel trail used for horses became visible through a clearing. It added a touch of Old Virginia to our walk.

The open fields were painted a frosty white and leafless trees stood tall against the solid blue sky. The only other color was the bright red from the cardinals hidden in the bramble that lined the trail.

"Every time I see a cardinal I think of Rhoda," Dad noted.

Why's that? I asked.

"Well, your Uncle Lou always called her "Red." You see, in her younger days she had a streak of red down the center of her hair, like the tuft of a male cardinal. He was the only one who ever called her that, and she got such a kick out of it.

"Did you know that we lived with Aunt Jean and Uncle Lou for the first six months of our marriage?"

No. Why was that?

"You see, this was after I got out of the service, while I attended the University of Maine. They helped us out. They liked having Rhoda around: She'd spent almost every summer with them since she was thirteen. We moved out when I entered law school in Boston."

Dad pointed to several cardinals as they flew overhead.

"Do you think they're following us?"

We continued down the path. After a while I asked, Does your formula for happiness still work given the events of September 11th?

"Absolutely," he insisted, without hesitation. "People are resilient. America is resilient, and I can only see better days ahead."

Better days? I questioned.

"Well, perhaps not immediately. The beauty of resilience is that it helps us to weather the storm, but I don't expect a lot of things to change. What I have witnessed, beyond the sheer pain of it all, is that the event, which demonstrated the worst part of humanity, has also brought out the best. I have witnessed Americans working side by side, helping those in pain. I have seen the pictures from around the world of hundreds of thousands of people laying flowers at American embassies and having prayer vigils asking for God's help for America.

"Nobody can tell the future, but like Pearl Harbor, September 11th could be a turning point for America. The bombing of Pearl Harbor awoke a sleeping giant, and America was dragged into World War II. As a result, the world was saved from fascism. Pearl Harbor served an important purpose for America and the world. Similarly, the tragic loss that America suffered that September day will not be in vain. Someday, maybe fifty years from now, that event will be regarded as an important day for America when viewed against the backdrop of history. But change doesn't occur overnight. Other than being more anxious, I don't expect things to be much different day to day.

"Remember, we don't live in the Garden of Eden. We live in a world where there is pain. There is suffering and there is sacrifice. America has sacrificed in the past, is sacrificing now, and will sacrifice in the future. We can overcome any challenge, but the reward of freedom does not come without sacrifice. Freedom isn't free."

What do you think will happen? I asked.

"I can only predict that in the long run we will be better off. Perhaps we will be forced to confront the kind of desperation that led to this hatred. Perhaps we will be safer because of the stronger security measures that will be put in place. Maybe the only benefit will be that people will modify their behavior and be a little nicer to each other. I don't know.

"Most of all, I have hope. I hope to see a day when people will be open-minded to all religions and appreciate those that encourage fair treatment and kindness. I also hope to see a day when those who are desperate refuse to act with violence in the name of God. Gandhi chose a non-violent path, as did Martin Luther King and Nelson Mandela. These individuals invoked the name of God on behalf of justice and fairness and were rewarded for their efforts. This is my hope for those who suffer.

"Still, *Attunement* tells me to grieve for the families who have lost loved ones and accept that dark hours like these are part of a larger plan."

What do you mean by attunement?

"Attunement is spiritual guidance, intuition, or what I believe is the connection to the Cosmic Pattern. Attunement is reached by mastering one's feelings and actions," Dad said.

"Let me back up for a minute. There's a better way to explain it."

Then he put his hand to his ear and asked, "Did you hear that?"

Hear what? I asked.

"Did you hear one of the thousands of radio waves that are around us right now as we speak?"

Then after a pause, he answered his own question.

"Of course not. In order to hear any of those things you're going to need the right equipment, like a radio, television, or telephone for that matter. But, just because you can't hear it doesn't mean it's not there.

"It's the same thing with attunement," he insisted, "but it's a lot more precise and usually goes unnoticed by most people. Similarly, you'll need equipment; in this case, your heart, your mind, and your soul. In order to tap into the message, you'll need to be plugged in spiritually and tuned in with a peaceful mind. Most importantly, you've got to be listening with your heart for intuitive feelings," Dad emphasized.

What does attunement do for you? Can it predict the future? I asked.

"Attunement is there for guidance and avoids trying to predict the future. In fact, you've got to be very cautious not to read too much into its message. Attunement is there to stimulate and inspire our spiritual capacity. It's what connects the physical with the spiritual, something I do through contemplation and prayer. But like any skill, it must be developed. I've found my own way to get the most out of it."

Why should anyone seek attunement? I asked.

"First, attunement is a privilege. It's a spiritual partnership there to enhance your life. So, if it's available to you, I ask, why wouldn't you want it? Why cheat yourself? Why not explore the possibilities? However, attunement is delicate and its message can easily be missed," Dad cautioned.

How come?

"The biggest culprit is greed. In order to attune, you must restrain from greed," Dad insisted.

What's wrong with accumulating wealth?

"I'm glad you brought that up. I think a lot of people get confused on this subject. Sure it's nice to have wealth. There's nothing wrong with it. But it's important to be able to keep things in balance. How many people do you know who are constantly searching for bigger and better cars or houses?

"Material possessions don't lead to happiness. Once a craving is satisfied, the novelty wears off and soon another craving arises—like an alcoholic, it never ends.

"Sure, we're all trying to fill voids in life. We're all trying to find answers for the emptiness we may have experienced along the way. Yet at some point, we must realize that neither money, nor Mercedes, can fill this void. Material possessions are only cosmetic and mask inner emptiness. True happiness is found by filling the void from the inside—not by covering it up," he stated.

"Wealth doesn't guarantee happiness. You see, I believe it's truly a curse not to be able to enjoy the things you have. Consider a millionaire who's not satisfied, who's envious of somebody richer. Is a millionaire happier than a person with limited means, who is content with fewer possessions?

"But don't get me wrong: It's okay to improve your circumstances. You can still become a Chief Executive Officer, make big money, and still be spiritual. I'm just recommending that you keep the desire for the material in balance. Don't get caught on the material treadmill," Dad said.

When did you learn how to keep it all in balance?

"It took me many years to find a balance between the spiritual and the material. Sure, I wanted a decent job, a comfortable place to live, and the ability to raise a family. I also wanted time for my writing. I wasn't renouncing material wealth. I didn't take a vow of poverty. I just refused to become a slave to the pursuit of material wealth. And it's worked for me.

"There's one more thing and it's a hard one to prove. But I genuinely had the feeling that if I did my part, enough material wealth would show up to satisfy my needs. And it always did," Dad said.

"I still have to do everything in my power to help myself. I understand that I can't expect to receive wisdom if I refuse to use my mind. I can't expect a healthy body if I live on junk food, smoke or don't exercise. I can't expect a paycheck if I haven't done an honest day's work. I always have to do my part."

What about prayer?

"Prayer helps you connect. You see, you can kid yourself, you can kid others, you can deny and even lie, but those who truly follow the spiritual path of attunement must remain honest with God. You can't lie to God, even if you want to. It's impossible. In my opinion, whether you pray in a church, a synagogue, a mosque, a temple, or in the privacy of your own home, the humility of prayer is what allows you to connect to the spiritual.

"Still, I want to go back to something you said earlier; you essentially asked, *What's in it for me?* My answer is simply this: Attunement is part of life. You're not doing it because there is a specific payoff. I don't say, okay, I'm going to do these ten or twenty things, lead a constructive life of high morality and expect a payoff. I can't expect a payoff. That violates the rules of attunement. No. I seek attunement because it's the spiritual path I've chosen—the way I want to live and the person I want to be.

"Of course, having said this, there are benefits that I receive from attunement. I believe it enhances my peace of mind and removes most of life's tension and frustration. Most of all, attunement provides spiritual guidance. I'm convinced of it."

How do you know you've had spiritual guidance?

"I don't. I believe that spiritual guidance accounts for many of the so-called coincidences that have occurred in my life. I see coincidence as the spiritual forces indirectly revealing themselves."

When did you begin to feel this way?

"It all really started when I fell down the elevator shaft, when I heard that voice saying, *Relax, everything is going to be all right.* I'd had many prior coincidences in my life, like most people. But while in that hospital bed after my fall, I thought about the number of coincidences that had occurred in my life. Seemingly random, the pattern was beyond my comprehension.

But, I thought, wait a minute; these are not just merely coincidences. That's when I became convinced that I wasn't just lucky, but this happened because I was spiritually attuned. It wasn't because I was a great guy, but merely because I worked on attunement.

"Over the years I've discovered that attunement is very subtle. It helps me recognize signposts that may be there to guide my journey. When I'm at a crossroads, attunement allows me to ask, what's the message here?"

Does this mean you believe in fate?

"If you're defining fate as predetermination, then no, I don't believe our lives are determined for us. Nor do I believe the other extreme, that we are merely the products of random chance. It's somewhere in the middle. We're guided in a constructive direction and still able to maintain our free will.

"I think I told you about how I got my various assignments in the military, simply by bumping into the right people at the right time. In fact, throughout my entire life, an outside observer would say I've been lucky. But I don't believe in luck. I believe in doing my part and by doing so the spiritual forces come through for me, even at the very edge of the precipice.

"Was it just good luck that I happened upon a summer course that changed my life? Was it just good luck that I fell down an elevator shaft and didn't even get a concussion or a broken bone? Was it just good luck when I had gastritis and a nurse happened to save my life in the middle of the night or that I healed the next day without needing surgery? How about being able to send you kids to private school because of the generosity of another and not paying one dime more than we could afford? This wasn't luck. These weren't just coincidences. This was the power of attunement."

How about the coincidence of my telephone call the night you were about to throw away your book? I asked him.

"That was no coincidence," he said with a smile. "That was attunement."

We had walked a couple of miles and it was time to turn around. On the way back we had to climb a steep hill. Dad had to stop halfway up to catch his breath. I took a moment and looked at him. His hair was graying. He had hearing aids, trifocals, high blood pressure and an assortment of minor ailments.

And sensing my concern he said, "I've realized that I've got to take it easier on the hills these days."

I saw a cardinal pecking on the ground not far away as Dad reached into his pocket and pulled out his *little black book*. Flipping through the pages, he found what he was looking for, something he'd written that he wanted to share with me.

After a moment he said, "You know, I don't claim to have all the spiritual answers, nobody does, but I offer these thoughts to assist you on your journey. I want you to know something," and he paused again, still trying to catch his breath.

Then he repeated, "I want you to know that I've come to accept death and the threat of death as an absolute indisputable fact. Even so, I believe and ask you to believe, that neither death, nor endless space, nor endless time, nor anyone or anything else can ever take away your faith and mission in life. I want you to know that the goodness, the kindness and the happiness, the constructive and satisfying feelings and self-expression, the spiritual wealth, love, satisfaction, inspiration, and attunement are available to you, or anyone, for that matter, who chooses this path and shares it with others.

"Most assuredly, these items can fill your life and cause it to overflow with a depth and richness of purpose and inspiration. Spiritual wealth like this makes an indelible mark upon you, upon time and upon anyone whom it touches, a mark that can never be erased in this life and throughout eternity, and having such spiritual wealth is my wish for you."

I considered his remarks as I watched the cardinal fly away, thinking to myself, *someday Dad's not going to be around to give me advice. I hope I'm prepared.*

Then I asked, Do you think you'll be able to contact me after you leave this world?

"I'm planning on it. Not only do I believe I can, I genuinely believe I will," he said confidently. "I can understand your desire to share your success in life with me. I want you to know, in spite of my age, that whether I am here with you on this earth, or in the spiritual world, I will always be with you to share your success. Perhaps, after I'm gone, when you see a cardinal you'll be reminded of my spirit. You'll know that I'm never that far away.

"And if I could offer you one piece of advice to carry with you, it would be this:

> *The art of living*
> *Is the art of giving.*
> *So give with love and*
> *Be close to God."*

Is that the secret to happiness?

He mulled over my question for a moment.

"Don't spend too much time searching for happiness. It's fruitless. Instead, understand that happiness, like attunement, is subtle and that the secret to happiness is realizing that happiness is an unintended consequence of how you live your life. By consistently practicing the *Art of Living,* you'll discover that happiness finds you."

As our walk neared its end I asked, Do you think happiness has again found you?

"There's no question about it."

You know, Dad, I think your *Art of Living* is quite valuable.

"Really, Young Fella," he acknowledged. "Maybe I should consider giving myself another raise."

This book was a gift from my dad. If you enjoyed reading it, please consider giving a copy to your friends. It is available at fine bookstores, or for a signed copy go to:

www.happyonseven.com.

If you have a personal success story you want to share, please send your thoughts to: harley@happyonseven.com

Thank You, Harley